# Idaho Mining Rights

*A Legal Guide for Miners, Prospectors, Investors and all others
Interested in the Mineral Lands of Idaho*

*by Orville E. Jackson
of the Idaho State Bar*

**with an introduction by Kerby Jackson**

# *Introduction*

It has often been said that "*gold is where you find it*", but even beginning prospectors understand that their chances for finding something of value in the earth or in the streams of the Golden West are dramatically increased by going back to those places where gold and other minerals were once mined by our forerunners. Despite this, much of the contemporary information on local mining history that is currently available is mostly a result of mere local folklore and persistent rumors of major strikes, the details and facts of which, have long been distorted. Long gone are the old timers and with them, the days of first hand knowledge of the mines of the area and how they operated. Also long gone are most of their notes, their assay reports, their mine maps and personal scrapbooks, along with most of the surveys and reports that were performed for them by private and government geologists. Even published books such as this one are often retired to the local landfill or backyard burn pile by the descendents of those old timers and disappear at an alarming rate. Despite the fact that we live in the so-called "Information Age" where information is supposedly only the push of a button on a keyboard away, true insight into mining properties remains illusive and hard to come by, even to those of us who seek out this sort of information as if our lives depend upon it. Without this type of information readily available to the average independent miner, there is little hope that our metal mining industry will ever recover.

This important volume and others like it, are being presented in their entirety again, in the hope that the average prospector will no longer stumble through the overgrown hills and the tailing strewn creeks without being well informed enough to have a chance to succeed at his ventures.

Kerby Jackson
Josephine County, Oregon
May 2018

# GOLD RUSH BOOKS

OREGON, USA

www.GoldMiningBooks.com

# CONTENTS.

# EXPLANATORY,

The great industry of Idaho in the future and the one which today holds out the brighest and most alluring prospects of profit to the investor, creating the broadest field for the energies and talent of the laboring and business people of the State of Idaho, and a sure and high priced market for the greater part of her agricultural, horticultural and dairy products, is that of mining.

Since the publication of the first edition of "Idaho Mining Rights" in the year 1899, the work has become so popular with the prospector and mining man in the State of Idano and so highly approved by them as well as by the legal profession as evidenced by the speedy sale of a second edition, that the publication of a third edition is now being demanded by the mining public. "Idaho Mining Rights" in its third edition needs no introduction to the mining men of the State of Idaho. It has been probably well said that "Idaho Mining Rights" has done more to save to the mining and prospecting fraternity, the beneficient results of their hard labors performed in their efforts to uncover the valuable mineral treasures of the State of Idaho, than any book ever published on the subject, and it is the hope of the Author, that this, the third and Revised Edition of the work may prove equally useful to our mining people as well as constitute a ready book of re'erence for the legal fraternity, as to practical questions on mining law therein treated.

In closing, the Author has but one suggestion to make to those who have occasion to use this book, and that is, that it is not written to instruct anybody as to how he may evade the law, or how nearly he may comply with the law and yet not meet all of its requirements, but rather how he may fully comply with the law and thereby keep as far as possible from the precipice of danger of losing what he has endured much of hardship to acquire and probably expended much money to retain and develop.

Respectfully,

ORVILLE E. JACKSON,

The Author.

# IDAHO MINING RIGHTS.

## CHAPTER I.

### Statutes of the United States, Pertaining to Mineral Lands, Etc.

In reading and studying the statutes of this chapter, the miner must always bear in mind that the United States laws are paramount. That is to say, that the conditions by their provisions imposed on those desiring to locate and hold mining claims must be complied with and followed and cannot be removed by State law, although the State may add to them by legislation.

### MINERAL LANDS RESERVED FROM SALE UNDER PRE-EMPTION ACTS.

Section 2318. In all cases lands valuable for minerals shall be reserved from sale, except as otherwise expressly directed by law. (Sec. 5 of Act of July 4, 1866.)

### RIGHTS OF LOCATION AND DISTRICT RULES.

Section 2319. All valuable mineral deposits in lands belonging to the United States, both surveyed and unsurveyed, are hereby declared to be free and open to exploration and purchase, and the lands in which they are found, to occupation and purchase, by citizens of the United States and those who have declared their intention to become such, under regulations prescribed by law, and according to the local customs or rules of miners in the several mining districts, so far as the same are applicable and not inconsistent with the laws of the United States. (Sec. 1, Act of May 10, 1872.)

### LENGTH AND WIDTH OF CLAIMS—DISCOVERY OF VEIN OR LODE REQUIRED.

Section 2320. Mining claims upon veins or lodes of quartz or other rock in place, bearing gold, silver, cinnibar, lead, tin, copper, or other valuable deposits, heretofore located, shall be governed as to length along the vein or lode by the customs, regulations and laws in force at the date of their location. A mining claim located after the tenth day of May, eighteen hundred and seventy-two, whether located by one or more persons, may equal, but shall not exceed one thousand five hundred feet in length along the vein or lode; but no location of a mining claim shall be made until the discovery of the vein or lode within the limits of the claim located. No claim shall extend more than three hundred feet on each side of the middle of the vein at the surface, nor shall any claim be limited by any mining regulation to less than twenty-five feet on each side of the middle of the vein at the surface, except where adverse rights existing on the tenth day of May, eighteen hundred and seventy-two, render such limitation necessary. The end lines of each claim shall be parallel to each other. (Sec. 2, Act of May 10, 1872.)

## PROOF OF CITIZENSHIP OF INDIVIDUAL AND CORPORATION CLAIMANTS.

Section 2321. Proof of citizenship, under this chapter, may consist, in case of an individual of his own affidavit thereof; in the case of an association of persons unincorporated, of the affidavit of their authorized agent, made on his own knowledge, or upon information and belief; and in the case of a corporation organized under the laws of the United States, or of any State or Territory thereof, by the filing of a certified copy of their charter or certificate of incorporation. (Sec. 7 of Act of May 10, 1872.)

## APEX, SURFACE, DIP, AND OTHER VEINS WITHIN LOCATION OF CLAIM.

Section 2322. The locators of all mining locations heretofore made or which shall hereafter be made, on any mineral vein, lode or ledge, situated on the public domain, their heirs and assigns, where no adverse claim exists on the tenth day of May, eighteen hundred and seventy-two, so long as they comply with the laws of the United States and with the State, Territorial, and local regulations not in conflict with the laws of the United States governing their possessory title, shall have the exclusive right of possession and enjoyment of all the surface included within the lines of their locations and of all the veins, lodes and ledges throughout their entire depth, the top or apex of which lies inside of such surface lines extended downward vertically, although such veins, lodes or ledges may so far depart from a perpendicular in their course, downward as to extend outside the vertical side lines of such surface locations. But their right of possession to such outside parts of such veins or ledges shall be confined to such portions thereof as lie between vertical planes drawn downward as above described, through the end lines of their locations, so continued in their own direction that such planes will intersect such exterior parts of such veins or ledges. And nothing in this section shall authorize the locator or possessor of a vein or lode which extends in its downward course beyond the vertical lines of his claim to enter upon the surface of a claim owned or possessed by another. (Sec. 3 of Act of May 10, 1872.)

## TUNNELS.

Section 2323. Where a tunnel is run for the development of a vein or lode, or for the discovery of mines, the owners of such tunnel shall have the right of possession of all veins or lodes within three thousand feet from the face of such tunnel on the line thereof, not previously known to exist, discovered in such tunnel, to the same extent as if discovered from the surface; and locations on the line of such tunnel of veins or lodes not appearing on the surface, made by other parties after the commencement of the tunnel, and while the same is being prosecuted with reasonable diligence, shall be invalid: but failure to prosecute the work on the tunnel for six months shall be considered as an abandonment of the right to all undiscovered veins on the line of such tunnel. (Sec. 4 of Act of May 10, 1872.)

## DISTRICT RULES, LOCATION RECORD, ANNUAL LABOR AND FORFEITURE.

Section 2324. The miners of each mining district may make regulations not in conflict with the laws of the United States, or with the laws of the State or Territory in which the district is situated governing the location, manner of recording, amount of work necessary to hold possession of a mining claim, subject to the following requirements: The location must be distinctly marked on the ground so that its boundaries can be readily traced. All records of mining claims hereafter made shall contain the name or names of the locators, the date of the location, and such a description of the claim or claims located by reference to some natural object or permanent monument as will identify the claim. On each claim located after the tenth day of May, eighteen hundred and seventy-two, and until a patent has been issued therefor, not less than one hundred dollars' worth of labor shall be performed or improvements made during each year. On all claims located prior to the tenth day of May, eighteen hundred and seventy-two, ten dollars' worth of labor shall be performed or improvements made by the tenth day of June, eighteen hundred and seventy four and each year thereafter, for each one hundred feet in length along the vein until a patent has been issued therefor; but where such claims are held in common, such expenditure may be made upon any one claim, and upon a failure to comply with these conditions, the claim or mine upon which such failure occurred shall be open to relocation in the same manner as if no location of the same had ever been made, provided that the original locators, their heirs, assigns or legal representatives, have not resumed work upon the claim after failure and before such location. Upon the failure of any one of several co-owners to contribute his proportion of the expenditures required hereby, the co-owners who have performed the labor or made the improvements may, at the expiration of the year give such delinquent co-owner, personal notice in writing or notice by publication in the newspaper published nearest the claim, for at least once a week for ninety days, and if at the expiration of ninety days after such notice in writing or by publication, such delinquent should fail or refuse to contribute his proportion of the expenditure required by this section, his interest in the claim shall become the property of his co-owners who have made the required expenditures. (Sec. 5 of Act of May 10, 1872.)

**LABOR BY TUNNEL.** (Amendment of 1875 to Section 2324.)

That section two thousand three hundred and twenty-four, of the Revised Statutes be, and the same is hereby, amended so that where a person or company has or may run a tunnel for the purposes of developing a lode or lodes, owned by said person or company, the money so expended in said tunnel shall be taken and considered as expended on said lode or lodes, whether located prior to or since the passage of said act; and such person or company shall not be required to perform work on the surface of said lode or lodes in order to hold the same as required by said act. (Sec. 1 of Act of February 11, 1875.)

**ANNUAL LABOR.** (Amendment of 1880 to Section 2324.)

That section twenty-three hundred and twenty-four of the Revised Statutes of the United States be amended by adding the following words: "Provided, That the period within which the work required to be done annually on all unpatented mineral claims shall commence on the first day of January succeeding the date of location of such claim, and this section shall apply to all claims located since the tenth day of May, Anno Domini, eighteen hundred and seventy-two." (Sec. 2 of Act of January 22, 1880.)

## APPLICATION FOR PATENT.

Section 2325. A patent for any land claimed and located for valuable deposits may be obtained in the following manner: Any person, association, or corporation authorized to locate a claim under this chapter, having claimed and located a piece of land for such purposes, who has, or have, complied with the terms of this chapter, may file in the proper land office an application, for a patent under oath showing such compliance, together with a plat and field notes of the claim or claims in common made by or under the direction of the United States surveyor-general, showing accurately the boundaries of the claim or claims, which shall be distinctly marked by monuments on the ground, and shall post a copy of such plat, together with a notice of such application for a patent, in a conspicuous place on the land, embraced in such plat previous to the filing of the application for a patent, and shall file an affidavit of at least two persons, that such notice has been duly posted, and shall file a copy of the notice in such land office, and shall thereupon be entitled to a patent for the land, in the manner following: The Register of the Land Office, upon the filing of such application, plat, field notes, notices, and affidavits, shall publish a notice that such application has been made, for the period of sixty days, in a newspaper to be by him designated as published nearest to such claim; and he shall also post such notice in his office for the same period. The claimant at the time of filing this application or at any time thereafter, within the sixty days of publication, shall file with the Register, a certificate of the United States surveyor-general that five hundred dollars' worth of labor has been expended or improvements made upon the claim by himself or grantors, that the plat is correct, with such further description by such reference to natural objects or permanent monuments as shall identify the claim, and furnish an accurate description, to be incorporated in the patent. At the expiration of the sixty days of publication, the claimant shall file his affidavit, showing that the plat and notice have been posted in a conspicuous place on the claim during such period of publication. If no adverse claim shall have been filed with the Register and the Receiver of the proper land office at the expiration of the sixty days of publication, it shall be assumed that the applicant is entitled to a patent, upon the payment to the proper office of five dollars per acre, and that no adverse claim exists; and thereafter no objection from third parties to the issuance of a patent shall be heard, except it be shown that the applicant has failed to comply with the terms of this Chapter. (Sec. 6 of Act of May 10, 1872.)

## PATENT APPLICATION BY NON-RESIDENTS—(Amendment of 1880 to Section 2325, Revised Statutes of United States.)

That section twenty-three hundred and twenty-five of the Revised Statutes of the United States be amended by adding thereto, the following words: "Provided, That where the claimant for a patent is not a resident of, or within the land district, wherein the vein, lode, ledge or deposit sought to be patented is located, the application for patent and the affidavits required to be made in this section by the claimant for such patent may be made by his, her, or its authorized agent, where said agent is conversant with the facts sought to be established by said affidavits: And provided, That this section shall apply to all applications now pending for patents to mineral lands." (Sec. 1 of Act of January 22, 1880.)

## ADVERSE CLAIMS.

Section 2326. Where an adverse claim is filed during the period of publication, it shall be upon oath of the person or persons making the same, and shall show the nature, boundaries, and extent of such adverse claim and all proceedings except the publication of notice and making and filing the affidavit thereof, shall be stayed until the controversy shall have been settled or decided by a court of competent jurisdiction, or the adverse claim waived. It shall be the duty of the adverse claimant, within thirty days after filing his claim, to commence proceedings in a court of competent jurisdiction, to determine the question of the right of possession, and prosecute the same with reasonable diligence to final judgment; and a failure so to do shall be a waiver of his adverse claim. After such judgment shall have been rendered, the party entitled to the possession of the claim, or any portion thereof, may, without giving further notice, file a certified copy of the judgment roll with the Register of the Land Office, together with the certificate of the Surveyor-General that the requisite amount of labor has been expended or improvements made thereon, and the description required in other cases, and shall pay to the Receiver, five dollars per acre for his claim, together with the proper fees, whereupon the whole proceedings and the judgment roll shall be certified by the Register to the Commissioner of the General Land Office, and a patent shall issue thereon for the claim, or such portion thereof as the applicant shall appear from the decision of the Court, to rightly possess. If it appears from the decision of the Court that several parties are entitled to separate and different portions of the claim, each party may pay for his portion of the claim, with the proper fees, and file the certificate and description by the Surveyor-General whereupon the Register shall certify the proceedings and judgment roll to the Commissioner of the General Land Office as in the preceding case and patent shall issue to the several parties according to their respective rights. Nothing herein contained shall be construed to prevent the alienation of the title conveyed by a patent for a mining claim to any person whatever. (Sec. 7 of Act of May 10, 1872.)

## NEITHER PARTY PROVING TITLE.—(Amendment of 1881 to Section 2326, Revised Statutes, United States.)

That if in any action brought pursuant to section twenty-three hundred and twenty-six of the Revised Statutes, title to the ground in controversy shall not be established by either party, the jury shall so find, and judgment shall be entered according to the verdict. In such case costs shall not be allowed to either party, and the claimant shall not proceed in the land office or be entitled to a patent for the ground in controversy until he shall have perfected his title. (Act of March 3, 1881.)

## AGENT MAY ADVERSE FOR NON-RESIDENT.—(Amendment of 1882 to Section 2326, Revised Statutes of United States.)

That the adverse claim required by section twenty-three hundred and twenty-six of the Revised Statutes may be verified by the oath of any duly authorized agent or attorney in fact of the adverse claimant cognizant of the facts stated; and the adverse claimant, if residing or at the time, being beyond the limits of the district wherein the claim is situated, may make oath to the adverse claim before the clerk of any court of record of the United States or of the State or Territory where the adverse claimant may then be or before any notary public of such State or Territory. (Sec. 1 of Act of April 26, 1882.)

## AFFIDAVITS OUT OF LAND DISTRICT.—(Section 2 of Same Amendatory Act.)

That applicants for mineral patents, if residing beyond the limits of the district wherein the claim is situate, may make any oath or affidavit required for proof of citizenship before the clerk of any court of record or before any notary public of any State or Territory. (Sec. 2 of Act of April 26, 1882.)

## SURVEY.

Section 2327. The description of the vein or lode claims, upon surveyed lands, shall designate the location of the claim with reference to the lines of the public surveys, but need not conform therewith; but where a patent shall be issued for claims upon unsurveyed lands, the Surveyor-General, in extending the surveys shall adjust the same to the boundaries of such patented claim, according to the plat or description thereof, but so as in no case to interfere with or change the location of any such patented claim. (Sec. 8 of Act of May 10, 1872.)

## PREVIOUS APPLICATIONS.

Section 2328. Applications for patents for mining claims under former laws now pending, may be prosecuted to a final decision in the General Land Office, but in such cases where adverse rights are not affected thereby, patents may issue in pursuance of the provisions of this chapter; and all patents for mining claims upon the veins or lodes heretofore issued shall convey all the rights and privileges conferred by this chapter where no adverse rights existed on the tenth day of May, eighteen hundred and seventy-two. (Sec. 9 of Act of May 10, 1872.)

## PLACERS SUBJECT TO ENTRY.

Section 2329. Claims usually called "placers" including all forms of deposit, excepting veins of quartz or other rock in place shall be subject to entry and patent under like circumstances and conditions, and upon similar proceedings as are provided for vein or lode claims; but where the lands have been previously surveyed by the United States, the entry in its exterior limit shall conform to the legal subdivisions of the public lands. (Sec. 12 of Act of July 9, 1870.)

## LEGAL SUBDIVISION OF PLACERS.

Section 2330. Legal subdivisions of forty acres may be subdivided into ten acre tracts; and two or more persons or associations of persons, having contiguous claims of any size, although such claims may be less than ten acres each, may make joint entry thereof, but no location of a placer claim, made after the ninth day of July, eighteen hundred and seventy, shall exceed one hundred and sixty acres for any one person or association of persons, which location shall conform to the United States surveys, and nothing in this section contained shall defeat or impair any bona fide pre-emption or homestead claim upon agricultural lands, or authorize the sale of the improvements of any bona fide settler to any purchaser. (Sec. 12 of Act of July 9, 1870.)

## PLACERS ON SURVEYED LANDS.

Section 2331. Where placer claims are upon surveyed lands, and conform to legal subdivisions, no further survey or plat shall be required, and all placer mining claims located after the tenth day of May, eighteen hundred and seventy-two, shall conform as near as practicable with the United States system of public land surveys, and the rectangular subdivisions of such surveys, and no such location shall include more than twenty acres for each individual claimant; but where placer claims cannot be conformed to legal subdivisions, survey and plat shall be made as on unsurveyed lands; and where by the segregation of mineral lands in any legal subdivision a quantity of agricultural land less than forty acres remains, such fractional portion of agricultural land may be entered by any party qualified by law for homestead or pre-emption purposes. (Sec. 10 of Act of May 10, 1872.)

## LIMITATIONS.

Section 2332. Where such person or association, they, or their grantors, have held and worked their claims for a period equal to the time prescribed by the Statute of Limitations for mining claims of the State or Territory where the same may be situated, evidence of such possession and working of the claims for such period shall be sufficient to establish a right to a patent thereto under this chapter, in the absence of any adverse claim, but nothing in this chapter shall be deemed to impair any lien which may have attached in any way whatever to any mining claim or property thereto attached prior to the issuance of a patent. (Sec. 13 of Act of July 9, 1870.)

## PLACER CLAIM EMBRACING LODE.

Section 2333. Where the same person, association or corporation is in possession of a placer claim, and also a vein or lode included within the boundaries thereof, application shall be made for a patent for the placer claim, with the statement that it includes such vein or lode and in such case a patent shall issue for the placer claim, subject to the provisions of this chapter, including such vein or lode, upon the payment of five dollars per acre for such vein or lode claim, and twenty-five feet of surface on each side thereof. The remainder of the placer claim, or any placer claim not embracing any vein or lode claim, shall be paid for at the rate of two dollars and fifty cents per acre, together with all costs of proceedings; and where a vein or lode, such as is described in section twenty-three hundred and twenty, is known to exist within the boundaries of a placer claim, an application for a patent for such placer claim, which does not include an application for the vein or lode claim shall be construed as a conclusive declaration that the claimant of the placer claim has no right of possession of the vein or lode claim; but where the existence of a vein or lode in a placer claim is not known, a patent for the placer claim shall convey all valuable mineral and other deposits within the boundaries thereof. (Sec. 11 of Act of May 10, 1872.)

## DEPUTY SURVEYOR, FEES AND CHARGES FOR PUBLICATION.

Section 2334. The Surveyor-General of the United States may appoint in each land district containing mineral lands, as many competent surveyors as shall apply for appointment to survey mining claims. The expenses of the survey of vein or lode claims, and the survey and subdivision of placer claims into smaller quantities than one hundred and sixty acres, together with the cost of publication of notices, shall be paid by the applicants, and they shall be at liberty to obtain the same at the most reasonable rates, and they shall also be at liberty to employ any United States Deputy Surveyor to make the survey. The Commissioner of the General Land Office shall also have the power to establish the maximum charges for surveys and publication of notices under this chapter; and in case of excessive charges for publication he may designate any newspaper published in a land district where mines are situated for the publication of mining notices in such district, and fix the rates to be charged by such paper; and, to the end that the Commissioner may be fully informed on the subject, each applicant shall file with the Register, a sworn statement of all charges and fees paid by such applicant for publication and surveys, together with all fees and money paid the Register and Receiver of the land office, which statement shall be transmitted, with the other papers in the case, to the Commissioner of the General Land Office. (Sec. 12 of Act of May 10, 1872.)

### AFFIDAVITS, PROOFS AND AGRICULTURAL CONTESTS.

Section 2335. All affidavits required to be made under this chapter may be verified before any officer authorized to administer oaths within the land district where the claims may be situated, and all testimony and proofs may be taken before any such officer, and when duly certified by the officer taking the same, shall have the same force and effect as if taken before the Register and Receiver of the land office. In cases of contest as to the mineral or agricultural character of land, the testimony and proofs may be taken as herein provided on personal notice of at least ten days to the opposing party, or if such party cannot be found, then by publication of at least once a week for thirty days in a newspaper, to be designated by the Register of the Land Office as published nearest to the location of such land; and the Register shall require proof that such notice has been given. (Sec. 13 of Act of May 10, 1872.)

### CROSS VEINS AND VEINS UNITING ON THEIR DIP.

Section 2336. Where two or more veins intersect or cross each other, priority of title shall govern, and such prior location shall be entitled to all ore or mineral contained within the space of intersection; but the subsequent location shall have the right of way through the space of intersection for the purposes of the convenient working of the mine. And where two or more veins unite, the oldest prior location shall take the vein below the point of union, including all the space of intersection. (Sec. 14 of Act of May 10, 1872.)

### MILL SITES.

Section 2337. Where non-mineral land not contiguous to the vein or lode is used or occupied by the proprietor of such vein or lode for mining or milling purposes, such non-adjacent surface ground may be embraced and included in an application for a patent for such vein or lode, and the same may be patented therewith, subject to the same preliminary requirements as to survey and notice as are applicable to veins or lodes; but no location hereafter made of such non-adjacent land shall exceed five acres, and payment for the same must be made at the same rate as fixed by this chapter for the superficies of the lode. The owner of a quartz mill or reduction works, not owning a mine in connection therewith, may also receive a patent for his mill site, as provided in this section. (Sec. 15 of Act of May 10, 1872.)

## EASEMENTS.

Section 2338. As a condition of sale, in the absence of necessary legislation by Congress, the local Legislature of any State or Territory may provide rules for working such mines, involving easements, drainage and other necessary means to their complete development, and those conditions shall be fully expressed in the patent. (Sec. 5 of Act of July 26, 1866.)

## APPROPRIATION OF WATER RIGHTS.

Section 2339. Whenever, by priority of possession, rights to the use of water for mining, agricultural, manufacturing, or other purpose, have vested and accrued, and the same are recognized and acknowledged by the local customs, laws, and the decisions of courts, the possessors and owners of such vested rights shall be maintained and protected in the same; and the right-of-way for the construction of ditches and canals for the purposes herein specified is acknowledged and confirmed; but whenever any person, in the construction of any ditch or canal, injures or damages the possession of any settler on the public domain, the party committing such injury or damage shall be liable to the party injured for such injury or damage. (Sec. 9 of Act of July 26, 1866.)

## PATENTS SUBJECT TO WATER DITCH AND RESERVOIR RIGHTS.

Section 2340. All patents granted or pre-emption or homesteads allowed shall be subject to any vested and accrued water right, or rights to ditches and reservoirs used in connection with such water rights, as may have been acquired under or recognized by the preceding section. (Sec. 17 of Act of July 9, 1870.)

## HOMESTEADS.

Section 2341. Wherever, upon the lands heretofore designated as mineral lands, which have been excluded from survey and sale, there have been homesteads made by citizens of the United States, or persons who have declared their intentions to become citizens, which homesteads have been made, improved and used for agricultural purposes, and upon which there have been no valuable mines of gold, silver, cinnabar, or copper discovered, and which are properly agricultural lands, the settlers or owners of such homesteads shall have a right of pre-emption thereto, and shall be entitled to purchase the same at the price of one dollar and twenty-five cents per acre, and in quantity not to exceed one hundred and sixty acres; or they may avail themselves of the provisions of Chapter five of this Title relating to Homesteads. (Sec. 10 of Act of July 26, 1866.)

## LAND DISTRICTS.

Section 2343. The President is authorized to establish additional land districts and to appoint the necessary officers under existing laws, wherever he may deem the same necessary for the public convenience in executing the provisions of this chapter. (Sec. 7 of Act of July 26, 1866.)

## STATE AND RAILROAD GRANTS.

Section 2346. No Act passed at the first session of the Thirty-Eighth Congress, granting lands to States or Corporations to aid in the construction of roads or for other purposes, or to extend the time of grants made prior to the thirtieth day of January, eighteen hundred and sixty-five, shall be so construed as to embrace mineral lands, which in all cases are reserved exclusively to the United States, unless otherwise especially provided in the Act or Acts making the grant. (Res. 10, January 30, 1865.)

## POSSESSORY ACTION.

Section 910. No possessory action between persons, in any court of the United States, for the recovery of any mining title, or for damages to such title, shall be affected by the fact that the paramount title to the land in which such mines lie, is in the United States; but each case should be adjudged by the laws of possession. (Sec. 9 of Act of February 27, 1865.)

## EXEMPTING VOLUNTEERS IN THE WAR WITH SPAIN FROM THE REQUIREMENTS OF SEC. 2324, REVISED STATUTES, U. S.

That the provisions of section twenty-three hundred and twenty-four of the Revised Statutes of the United States, which require that on each claim located after the tenth day of May, eighteen hundred and seventy-two, and until patent has been issued therefor, not less than one hundred dollars' worth of labor shall be performed or improvements made during each year, shall not apply to claims owned by persons who may enlist in the volunteer army of the United States for service in a war between this country and Spain, so that no mining claims owned by such person which has been regularly located and recorded as required by the local laws and mining regulations shall be subject to forfeiture for non-performance of the annual assessment during the time such owner is in the military service of the Government as aforesaid. (Act of Congress of 1898.)

## STATUTES OF THE UNITED STATES RELATING TO COAL LANDS.

### RIGHT TO ENTER—PRICE PER ACRE.

Section 2347. Every person above the age of twenty-one years, who is a citizen of the United States, or who has declared his intentions to become such, or any association of persons severally qualified as above, shall, upon application to the Register of the proper land office, have the right to enter, by legal subdivisions, any quantity of vacant coal-lands of the United States not otherwise appropriated or reserved by competent authority, not exceeding one hundred and sixty acres to such individual person, or three hundred and twenty acres to such association, upon payment to the Receiver of not less than ten dollars per acre, for such lands, where the same shall be situated more than fifteen miles from any completed railroad, and not less than twenty dollars per acre for such lands as shall be within fifteen miles of such road.

### PREFERENCE TO SETTLERS.

Section 2348. Any person or association of persons severally qualified as above provided, who have opened and improved, or shall hereafter open and improve, any coal mine or mines upon the public lands, and shall be in actual possession of the same, shall be entitled to a preference-right of entry, under the preceding section, of the mines so opened and improved; Provided, That when any association of not less than four persons, severally qualified as above provided, shall have expended not less than five thousand dollars in working and improving any such mine or mines, such association may enter not exceeding six hundred and forty acres, including such mining improvements.

### CLAIMS—WHEN TO BE PRESENTED.

Section 2349. All claims under the preceding section must be presented to the Register of the proper land district within sixty days after the date of actual possession and the commencement of improvements on the land, by the filing of a declaratory statement therefor; but when the township plat is not on file at the date of such improvement, filing must be made within sixty days from the receipt of such plat at the district office; and where the improvements shall have been made prior to the expiration of three months from the third day of March, eighteen hundred and seventy-three, sixty days from the expiration of such three months shall be allowed for the filing of a declaratory statement, and no sale under the provisions of this section, shall be allowed until the expiration of six months from the third day of March, eighteen hundred and seventy-three.

### BUT ONE ENTRY ALLOWED—FAILURE.

Section 2350. The three preceding sections shall be held to authorize only one entry by the same person or association of persons; and no association of persons any member of which shall have taken the benefit of such sections, either as individual or as a member of any other association, shall enter or hold any other lands under the provisions thereof, and no member of any association which shall have taken the benefit of such sections shall enter or hold any other lands under their provisions, and all persons claiming under section twenty three hundred and forty-eight, shall be required to prove their respective rights and pay for the lands filed upon within one year from the time prescribed for filing their respective claims; and upon failure to file the proper notice or to pay for the land within the required period, the same shall be subject to entry by any other qualified applicant.

### CONFLICTING CLAIMS—RULES AND REGULATIONS.

Section 2351. In case of conflicting claims upon coal lands where the improvements shall be commenced, after the third day of March, eighteen hundred and seventy-three, priority of possession and improvements, followed by proper filing and continued good faith, shall determine the preference right to purchase. And also where improvements have already been made prior to the third day of March, eighteen hundred and seventy-three, division of the land claimed may be made by legal subdivision, to include as near as may be, the valuable improvements of the respective parties. The Commissioner of the General Land Office is authorized to issue all needful rules and regulations for carrying into effect the provisions of this and the four preceding sections.

### MINERAL LANDS EXCEPTED.

Section 2352. Nothing in the five preceding sections shall be construed to destroy or impair any rights which may have attached prior to the third day of March, eighteen hundred and seventy-three, or to authorize the sale of lands valuable for mines of gold, silver or copper.

## OIL PLACER ACT.

That any person authorized to enter lands under the mining laws of the United States may enter and obtain patent to lands containing petroleum or other mineral oils, and chiefly valuable therefor, under the provisions of the laws relating to placer mineral claims: Provided, That lands containing such petroleum or other mineral oils which have heretofore been filed upon,-claimed, or improved as mineral, but not yet patented, may be held and patented under the provisions of this Act the same as if such filing, claim or improvement were subsequent to the date of the passage hereof.    (Act of Congress of February 11, 1897.)

## SALINE PLACER ACT.

That all unoccupied public lands of the United States containing salt springs, or deposits of salt in any form, and chiefly valuable therefor, are hereby declared to be subject to location and purchase under the provisions of the law relating to placer mining claims: Provided, That the same person shall not locate or enter more than one claim hereunder.  (Act of Congress January 31, 1901.)

# CHAPTER II.

### Statutes of the State of Idaho Relating to Mines, Being a Revision Up To Date of the Laws on the Subject, in Force and Effect.

### LOCATION OF LODE MINING CLAIMS.

Section 1.  Mining claims hereafter located upon veins or lodes of quartz or other rock in place bearing any of the metals or other valuable deposits mentioned in section 2320 of the Revised Statutes of United States, may extend to three hundred feet on each side of the middle of the vein or lode:  Provided, That when the locators have set stakes, posts or monuments described in Section 2 hereof, to indicate the line of the vein, ledge or lode, such stakes, posts or monuments must be taken for the purpose of such location, to mark correctly the line thereof, and such line must not afterwards be changed so as to affect rights acquired or interfere with any locations made subsequent thereto. (Sec. 1 of Act of March 5, 1895.  Re-enacted February 14, 1899.  Amending Section 3100, Revised Statutes.)

### DISCOVERY, NOTICE, BOUNDARIES, ETC.

Sec. 2.  The locator, at the time of making the discovery of such vein or lode, must erect a monument at such place of discovery, upon which he must place his name, the name of the claim, the date of discovery and distance claimed along the vein each way from such monument.  Within ten days after the date of the discovery, he must mark the boundaries of his claim by establishing at each corner thereof, and at any angle in the side lines, a monument marked with the name of the claim and the corner or angle it represents; also at the time of so marking his boundaries, he must post at his discovery monument his notice of location in which must be stated:

First.  The name of the locator.

Second.  The name of the claim.

Third.  The date of discovery.

Fourth.  The direction and distance claimed along the ledge from the discovery.

Fifth. The distance claimed on each side of the middle of the ledge.

Sixth. The distance and direction from the discovery monument, to such natural object or permanent monument, if any such there be, as will fix and describe in the notice itself, the location of the claim; and,

Seventh. The name of the mining district, County and State.

When from any cause a monument cannot be safely planted at the true corner or angle, it may be placed as near thereto as practicable, and so marked as to indicate the place of such corner or angle.

Monuments may be made of any such material or form as will readily give notice, and when of posts or trees, they must be hewn and marked upon the side facing towards the discovery, and must be at least four inches square or in diameter. Monuments must be at least four feet high above the ground, and trees must be so hewn as to readily attract attention. At the time the locator marks the boundaries of his claim, he may do so in any direction that will not interfere with rights or claims which existed prior to his discovery. (Section 1 of Act approved and in effect on the 13th day of March, 1899, Amending Section 2 of Act of March 5, 1895.)

## LOCATION. LABOR.

Sec. 3. Within sixty days after such location, the locator or his assigns, must sink a shaft upon the lode to the depth of at least ten feet from the lowest part of the rim of such shaft at the surface. And of not less than sixteen square feet area. Any excavation which shall cut such vein ten feet from the lowest part of the rim of such shaft and which shall measure one hundred and sixty cubic feet in extent shall be considered a compliance with this provision. Any located claim upon which work has been done in compliance with the above requirements is not, unless abandoned, subject to relocation for a period of ninety days from and after the date of location. (Sec. 3 of Act of March 5, 1895. Re-enacted February 14, 1899.)

## FILING OF NOTICE.

Sec. 4. Within ninety days after the location of the claim, the locator or his assigns must file for record in the office of the County Recorder of the County or of the Deputy Recorder of the mining district in which the claim is situated, a substantial copy of his notice of location. (Section 4 of Act of March 5, 1895. Re-enacted February 14, 1899. Amending Section 3103, Revised Statutes.)

## ADDITIONAL OR AMENDED CERTIFICATE OF LOCATION.

Sec. 5. If at any time the locator of any mining claim heretofore or hereafter located, or his assigns, shall apprehend that his original certificate was defective, erroneous, or that any of the requirements of the law had not been complied with before filing, or shall be desirous of changing the surface boundaries, or of taking any part of an overlapping claim which has been abandoned, or in case the original certificate was made prior to the passage of this law, and he shall be desirous of securing the benefits of this Act, such locator or his assigns, may file an additional certificate subject to the conditions of this Act and to contain all that this Act required an original certificate to contain: Provided, That such amended location does not interfere with the existing rights of others at the time when such amendment is made. (Sec. 5 of Act of March 5, 1895. Re-enacted February 14, 1899.)

## AFFIDAVIT.

Sec. 6. Within sixty days after any time set or period allowed for the performance of labor, or making improvements upon any lode or placer claim, the person in whose behalf such work or improvement is performed, or some person for him must make and record an affidavit in substance as follows:

State of Idaho, } ss.
County of .................... }

Before me the subscribed, personally appeared................... who being first duly sworn says that at least........................ dollars worth of work for improvements were performed or made upon ..........................claim situate in......................mining district, County of............State of Idaho. That such expenditure was made by, for, or at the expense of........................ owner of said claim for the purposes of holding said claim, and all stakes, monuments or trees marking boundaries of said claims are in proper place and position.

................................
Subscribed and sworn to before me this.....day of........190..

The foregoing affidavit is not so explicit in detail as it should be. I therefore offer and recommend the following form.—(The Author.)

State of Idaho,
County of...................... ss.

Before me the subscribed, personally appeared................... who being first duly sworn says that at least...............dollars worth of work for improvements were performed or made upon ........................claim, situate in...................mining district, County of......................State of Idaho, during the year A. D. 19.... That such expenditure was made by, for, or at the expense of........................owner of said claim for the purpose of holding said claim and as annual labor and improvements for said year 190....., and all stakes, monuments or trees marking boundaries of said claims are in proper place and position.

................................
Subscribed and sworn to before me this......day of........19...
................................
Notary Public.

The fee for administering the oath and recording the foregoing affidavit, when taken before the county recorder or Deputy Mining Recorder, shall be fifty cents; the fee for recording the same when the oath is taken before any other officer authorized to administer oaths shall be fifty cents. Such affidavit or a certified copy thereof in case the original is lost shall be prima facie evidence of the performance of such labor. The failure to file such affidavit shall be considered prima facie evidence that such labor has not been done. (Sec 2 of the Act of March 4, 1899.)

## LOCATION OF ABANDONED CLAIMS.

Sec. 7. The location of abandoned claims shall be done in the same manner as if the location were of a new claim; but the locator may instead of sinking a new discovery shaft, sink the original discovery shaft ten feet deeper than it was at the time of his location, or he may drive the open cut or tunnel ten feet further along the course of the lead, lode or vein, and must erect new posts or monuments. (Sec. 7 of Act of March 4, 1895. Re-enacted February 14, 1899.)

## LOCATION NOTICE WHEN VOID.

Sec. 8. No location notice shall claim more than one location, whether the location is made by one or several locators, and if it purport to claim more than one location it is absolutely void. (Sec. 8 of Act of March 5, 1895. Re-enacted February 14, 1899.)

## DEPUTY MINING RECORDER.

Sec. 9. For the convenience of prospectors and locators, the County Recorders of the several counties must appoint a deputy at any place where he may deem it necessary, and at all places more than twenty miles distant from an existing office whenever ten or more mining locators interested, petition for the appointment of a deputy. Upon failure of any Recorder to appoint a deputy for ten days after the petition in writing has been presented to him, the resident miners in such district may appoint temporarily, one of their members to act as the recorder for the district, whose record shall be as valid as if made by the deputy, and must be entered by the recorder as herein after required: Provided, That whenever at any time afterwards, the recorder has appointed a deputy for such district or place, the authority of the person elected by the resident miners ceases. (Sec. 9 of Act of March 5, 1895. Re-enacted February 14, 1899, and amending section 3103, Revised Statutes.)

## SECURITY AGAINST DAMAGE TO SURFACE.

Sec. 10. When the right to mine is in any case separate from the ownership or right of occupancy of the surface ground, the owners or rightful occupants of the surface ground may demand satisfactory security from the miners; and if it be refused or not given, may enjoin such miners from working such ground until such security is given. The court granting the writ of injunction shall fix the amount and nature of the security. (Sec. 10 of Act of March 5, 1895. Re-enacted February 14, 1899.)

## LOCATION OF PLACER CLAIMS.

Sec. 11. Placer claims as mentioned in section 2329 of the Revised Statutes of the United States, may be located for the purpose of mining deposits and precious stones after the discovery of such deposits. (Sec. 11 of Act of March 5, 1895. Re-enacted February 14, 1899. Repealing section 3120, Revised Statutes.)

## LOCATION STAKES OR MONUMENTS—RECORD.

Sec. 12. The locator of any placer mining claim located for the purpose of mining placer deposits or precious stones, must at the time of making the location, place a substantial post or monument as is required in the location of quartz claims at each corner of the location and must also post on one of the same, a notice of location containing the date of the location, the name of the locator, the name and dimensions of the claim, the mining district, (if any), and county in which the same is situated; and must also give the distance and direction from said post or monument to such natural object or permanent monument, if any such there be, as will fix and describe in the notice itself, the location of the claim. Within fifteen days after making the location, the locator must make an excavation upon the claim of not less than one hundred cubic feet, for the purpose of prospecting the same. Within thirty days after the location, the locator must file for record in the office of the County Recorder, or of the Deputy Recorder of the mining district in which the claim is situated, a substantial copy of his notice of location, to which must be attached an affidavit such as is required in the case of quartz claims. (Act of March 2, 1897. Re-enacted February 14, 1899, Amending Section 12, Act of March, 1895.)

## AFFIDAVIT OF LOCATION—RECORD.

Sec. 13. At or before the time of presenting a location notice for record, whether it be for a quartz or placer claim, one of the locators named in the same must make and subscribe an affidavit, in writing on or attached to the notice, substantially in the following form, to-wit:

State of Idaho,

County of....................⟩ ss.

I, ............................., do solemnly swear that I am a citizen of the United States of America (or have declared my intentions to become such), and that I am acquainted with the mining ground described in this notice of location, and herewith called the ...................................ledge, lode or claim; that ground and claim therein described or any part thereof has not, to the best of my knowledge and belief, been located according to the laws of the United States and of this State, or if so located, that the same has been abandoned or forfeited by reason of the failure of such former locators to comply in respect thereto, with the requirements of said laws, and (in the case of quartz claims) that I have opened new ground to the extent or depth of ten feet as required by the laws of Idaho.

Signature.................................

Subscribed and sworn to before me this......day of....A. D. 19..

Signature.................................

(Section 13 of Act of March 5, 1895. Re-enacted February 14, 1899, Amending Section 3104 and repealing Section 3122, Revised Statutes.)

## RECORDING LOCATION NOTICE—FEES.

Sec. 14. The location notice herein required to be recorded must be recorded by the deputy appointed for the district, or the person appointed for that purpose as above provided, (when the legal fee therefor is tendered) in a book to be kept for that purpose. Said book must be indexed with the names of all locators arranged in alphabetical order, according to the family or surname of each. The fee to be tendered for making such record, administering the oath to the locator and certifying the same, for indexing the names appearing on the notice, and to include recording the notice by the recorder as hereinafter required, and the indexing by said recorder and the deputy, is two dollars, which fee must be equally divided between the recorder and the deputy or the person acting under an election as hereinbefore provided, and no other additional sum of money must be demanded or received by either of them for any services connected with the recording of any location notice made pursuant to the requirements of this chapter. (Sec. 14 of Act of March 5, 1895. Re-enacted February 14, 1899. Amending Section 3105, Revised Statutes.)

## RECORDING OF LOCATION NOTICE WITH DEPUTY MINING RECORDER.

Sec. 15. It shall be the duty of the County Recorder of the several Counties of this State, within fourteen days after receiving them, to transmit to the Deputy Mining Recorder of the district wherein the claims are situated. all location notices, both quartz and placer. which shall not have been already recorded in the office of the Deputy Mining Recorder.

It shall be the duty of such Deputy Mining Recorder to record in his records, all such notices received by him and he shall receive as compensation therefor, from the Clerk sending them, one-half the fee authorized by law to be charged for the recording of mining claims. After recording such notices, the Deputy Mining Recorder shall return the same to the County Recorder. (Act of March 7, 1903. Approved by the Governor, March 11, 1903.)

## RIGHT OF WAY FOR TUNNEL.

Sec. 16. Any person or company who has or may hereafter have a tunnel or cross-cut, the mouth of which is located upon his own ground or upon ground in his lawful occupation, shall have the right to drive and continue the same through and across any located or patented claim in front of the mouth of such tunnel, but not to follow or drive upon the vein belonging to the owner of such claim. (Section 1 of Act approved and in effect March 15, 1899.)

## RIGHTS OF OWNER OF INTERSECTED CLAIM—FORFEITURE.

Sec. 17. Each tunnel or cross-cut may be driven and worked for the purpose of drainage and for the purpose of reaching and working mining ground of the tunnel owned beyond the intersected claim. The owner or owners of any vein or claim or claims so intersected, or his duly authorized agent. shall have the right to enter such tunnel upon application to the owner or owners or person in charge of said tunnel, without resorting to any process of law for the purpose of making a survey and inspecting such vein or veins as may be crossed within the boundary lines of such intersected claim, and if the owner or owners of such tunnel, by bulk heading, damming back or in any manner prevent the inspection or survey herein provided for, or if such owner or owners shall in any manner prevent the natural drainage of water from such intersected claim or claims without the consent of the owner or owners thereof, it shall work a forfeiture of all rights granted under Section 1, of this Act. (Section 2 of Act approved and in effect March 15, 1899.)

## ORE EXTRACTED—LIABILITY.

Sec. 18. If any ore. the property of the owner of the claim intersected or crossed, be extracted in the driving such tunnel, it shall be the property of the owner of the vein from which it was taken and the owner of the tunnel shall be liable for all actual damages or injury done to the owner of the claim crossed by his tunnel. (Section 3 of Act approved and in effect March 15, 1899.)

## ACTION—BURDEN OF PROOF.

Sec. 19. In all actions between the tunnel and others involving the right to any vein discovered in such tunnel, the burden of proving that the vein so discovered is not the property of the adverse claimant in such action. shall be on the tunnel owner. (Section 4 of Act approved and in effect March 15, 1899.)

## RIGHT OF WAY.

Sec. 20. The owner. locator or occupant of a mining claim, whether patented under the laws of the United States or held by location or possession, may have and acquire a right of way for ingress and egress, when necessary for working such mining claim, over and across the lands or mining claims of others, whether patented or otherwise. (Section 3130, Revised Statutes.)

## EASEMENT FOR ROAD, DITCH, ETC.

Sec. 21. When any mine or mining claim is so situated that for the more convenient enjoyment of the same, a road, railroad or tramway therefrom or a ditch or canal to convey water thereto, or a ditch or flume, cut or tunnel, to drain or convey the waters or tailings therefrom, or a tunnel or shaft may be necessary for the better workings thereof, which road, railroad, tramway, ditch, canal, flume, shaft, cut or tunnel may require the occupancy of lands or mining grounds, owned, occupied or possessed by others than the person or persons or body corporate, requiring an easement for any of the purposes described, the owner, or claimant or occupant of the mine or mining claim first above mentioned, is entitled to a right-of-way, entry and possession for all the uses and privileges for such railroad, tramway, ditch, canal, flume, cut, shaft or tunnel, in, upon, through and across such other lands or mining claims. upon compliance with the provisions of this chapter. (Section 3131, Revised Statutes.)

## PROCEDURE TO OBTAIN RIGHT OF WAY.

Sec. 22. When the owner, claimant, or occupant of any mine or mining claim desires to work the same, and it is necessary to enable him to do so successfully and conveniently, that he have a right of way for any of the purposes mentioned in the foregoing sections. If such right-of-way cannot be acquired by agreement with the claimant or owner of the lands or claims over, through, across or upon which he seeks to acquire such right-of-way, he may commence an action in the District Court in and for the County in which such right-of-way, or some part thereof, is situated, by filing a verified complaint containing a particular description of the character and extent of the right sought, a description of the mine or claim of the plaintiff, and of the mine or claim and lands to be affected by such right of way or privilege, with the name of the occupant or owner thereof. He may also set forth any tender of compensation that he may have made and demand the relief sought. (Section 1 of Act of February, 1899. Going into effect on the 6th day of May, 1899. Amending Section 3132, Revised Statutes.)

## ISSUANCE OF SUMMONS.

Sec. 23. Upon the filing of such complaint, the clerk must issue a summons as provided in other civil actions and the same must be served in the manner prescribed by law for service in ordinary actions. (Section 2 of Act of February, 1899. Amending Section 3133 Revised Statutes.)

## COMMISSIONERS TO HEAR TESTIMONY.

Sec. 24. At any time after the service of the summons, the plaintiff may upon ten days' notice to the defendant, apply to the District Court or the Judge thereof for the appointment of commissioners, to assess the damages resulting from the grant of such right of way. If upon the hearing of such motion, and the affidavit and proofs offered by the respective parties, the Judge shall be of the opinion that the plaintiff has made a prima facie case entitling him to the relief demanded in the complaint, or any part thereof, he shall appoint three commissioners, who must be disinterested persons, residents of the county, to assess the damages resulting to the claims, mines, or lands, of defendant. But if such commissioners are not applied for and appointed, or their award is not approved by the Judge or Court, or if an appeal is taken from their award as hereinafter provided, the action shall be tried and determined by the Court, and the provisions of the Code of Civil Procedure applicable thereto shall govern the proceedings therein as in other civil actions, either party shall be entitled to a jury trial and may move for a new trial and appeal as in other cases. (Section 3 of Act of February, 1899. Amending Section 3134, Revised Statutes.)

### OATH AND REPORT OF COMMISSIONERS.

Sec. 25. The commissioners so appointed must be sworn to faithfully and impartially discharge their duties and must proceed without unreasonable delay to examine the premises and assess the damages resulting from such right or privilege prayed for, and report the amount of the same to the Judge appointing them, and if such right-of-way affects the property of more than one person or company, such report must contain an assessment of damages to each company or person. (Section 3135, Revised Statutes.)

### REPORT WHEN SET ASIDE.

Sec. 26. For good cause shown, the Judge may set aside the report of such commissioners and appoint three other commissioners whose duty shall be the same as above mentioned. (Section 3136, Revised Statutes.)

### RIGHTS UPON PAYMENT OR TENDER.

Sec. 27. Upon the payment of the sum assessed as damages as aforesaid, to the persons to whom it is awarded, or a tender thereof to them, then the person petitioning as aforesaid is entitled to the right-of-way prayed for in his petition, and may immediately proceed to occupy the same and erect thereon such works and structure, and make therein such excavations as may be necessary to the use and enjoyment of the right of way so awarded. (Section 3137, Revised Statutes.)

### APPEAL.

Sec. 28. Appeals from the assessment of damages made by the commissioners may be made and prosecuted in the proper District Court by any party interested at any time within ten days after the filing of the report of the commissioners. A written notice of such appeal must be served upon the appellee in the same manner as summons are served in civil actions. The appellant must file with the Clerk of the Court to which the appeal is made, a bond with sureties to be approved by the Clerk in the amount of the assessment appealed from in favor of the appellee, conditioned that the appellant will pay any costs that may be awarded to the appellee, and abide any judgment that may be rendered in the cause. (Section 3138, Revised Statutes.)

### TRIAL ON APPEAL.

Sec. 29. An appeal brings before the District Court the necessity of the right-of-way or easement for the successful and convenient working of the mining claim, and the amount of damages; and upon such appeal the case must be tried anew, and either party is entitled to a jury. (Section 3139, Revised Statutes.)

## RIGHTS PENDING APPEAL.

Sec. 30. The prosecution of an appeal from the award of the commissioners or from the judgment of the District Court does not hinder, delay or prevent the plaintiff from exercising all the rights and privileges granted by the award of judgment, if he deposit with the Clerk of the District Court the full amount of the damages awarded or adjudged the defendant, and execute and deliver to the Clerk a bond with sufficient sureties to be approved by the Clerk, in an amount to be fixed by the Judge of the District Court, conditioned to pay to the defendant any additional amount, over and above the amount so deposited that defendant may recover, and all costs to which he may be entitled under the provisions of this chapter. At any time after such deposit and before the final determination of the action the defendant may, upon demand, receive from the Clerk the amount so deposited, but his acceptance of the same, or any part thereof, shall bar any further prosecution of the appeal and shall be deemed an acquiesence and consent to the award and judgment, and the defendant shall not be entitled to any costs subsequent to the deposit. (Section 4 of Act of February, 1899. Going into effect on the 6th day of May, 1899. Amending Section 3140. Revised Statutes.)

## COSTS AWARDED DEFENDANT.

Sec. 31. If the defendant recover judgment against the necessity of the easement or for fifty dollars more damages than the plaintiff has tendered to him as provided in the next section or for fifty dollars more damage than the commissioners or judgment of the District Court awarded him, he shall recover the costs of the appeal, otherwise he must pay all such costs. (Section 5 of Act of February, 1899. Going into effect on the 6th day of May, 1899. Amending Section 3141, Revised Statutes.)

Sec. 32. The costs and expenses of proceedings under the provisions of this chapter, except as herein otherwise provided, must be paid by the party making the application: Provided, That if the applicant before the commencement of such proceedings, has tendered to the parties owning or occupying the lands or mining claims, a sum equal to or more than the amount of damages recovered, all of the costs and expenses must be paid by the party or parties owning the lands or claims affected by such right-of-way and who appeared and resisted the claim of the applicant thereto. (Section 3142, Revised Statutes.)

## MINING CONTRACTS TO BE RECORDED.

Sec. 33. Written contracts relating to prospecting or mining or to the formation of a co-partnership for that purpose, when signed by the parties thereto and indorsed by at least one witness, may be recorded in the office of the County Recorder of the County, wherein it is proposed to prosecute the business of said co-partnership or where the property affected by such contract is situated. (Section 1 of Act of March, 1899.)

## EFFECT OF SUCH RECORD.

Sec. 34. Such record shall be constructive notice to all persons of the matter contained in such contract or co-partnership agreement (Section 2 of Act of March, 1899.)

## LAW OF TAXATION OF MINES AND MINING CLAIMS, IMPROVE. MENTS THEREON AND NET PROFITS DERIVED THEREFROM.

Sec. 35. All mines and mining claims, both placer and rock, in place containing or bearing gold, silver, copper, lead, coal or other valuable mineral or metal deposits after purchase thereof from the United States, shall be taxed at the price paid the United States therefor, unless the surface ground, or some part thereof of said mine or mining claim is used for other than mining purposes and has a separate and independent value for such other purposes, in which case said surface ground or any part thereof so used for other than mining purposes shall be taxed at its value for such other purposes, and all machinery used in mining and all property and surface improvements upon mines or mining claims, which have a value separate and independent of such mines or mining claims and the net annual proceeds of all mines and mining claims shall be taxed. (Section 1 of Act of February 17, 1903.)

Sec. 36. Every person, corporation or association engaged in mining upon any quartz vein or lode, or placer mining claim containing gold, silver, copper, lead, coal or other precious and valuable minerals or metals or mineral or metal deposits must between the first day of January and the first day of May, in each year, make out a statement of the net profits derived from the mining of said metals or minerals from each mine or mining claim owned or worked by such person, or from each group of mines or mining claims worked by a common system of development, during the year preceding the first day of January, such statement must be verified by the oath of such person or superintendent or managing agent of such corporation or association, who must deliver the same to the assessor of the county in which such mines are situated. (Section 2 of Act of February 17, 1903.)

Sec. 37. The assessor must prepare at the time of the preparation of the general assessment work, another assessment book called "The Assessment Book of the Net Profits of Mines," alphabetically arranged, in which must be listed the net profits of all the mines in his county and in which must be specified in separate columns and under appropriate heads:

(1). The name of the owner or owners of the mines.

(2). The name, description and location of the mine.

(3). The number of tons extracted during the year.

(4). The gross yield or value in dollars and cents.

(5). The actual cost of extracting the same from the mine.

(6). The actual cost of transportation to the place of reduction or sale.

(7). The actual cost of reduction or sale.

(8). The cost of construction of betterments and repair of mines and reduction works during the year.

(9). The net profits in dollars.

(10). The total amount of taxes. (Section 3 of Act of February 17, 1903.)

Sec. 38. The term "net profits" as employed in this act means the amount of money received from the mining of said metals or minerals from said mine or mining claim after the deduction of the actual expenditure of money and labor in and about extracting the metals and minerals from the mine or mining claim and transporting the same to the mill, concentrator or reduction works, and the reduction thereof, and the conversion of the same into money, or its equivalent, and also the deduction of all moneys expended for necessary labor, machinery and supplies needed and used in the mining operations, for the improvements necessary in and about the mine or mining claim for reducing ores, for the construction of the mills and reduction works, used and operated in connection with the mine or mining claim, for transporting the ore, and for extracting the metals and minerals therefrom, but the money invested in the mine or improvements made during any year except the year immediately preceding such statement must not be included therein. Such expenditures do not include the salaries, or any portion thereof, of any person or officers not actually engaged in the working of the mine or personally superintending the management thereof. (Section 4 of Act of February 17, 1903.)

Sec. 39. Where the same person or company or association is operating two or more mining claims, under one general system of mining or development, the product of which group of mines is mingled and treated as one mining operation, the statement of the owner provided herein to be made and the assessment provided herein to be made by the assessor shall be made as to such entire group, and need not be made as to each particular mining claim constituting said group. (Section 5 of Act of February 17, 1903.)

Sec. 40. The duties of the Assessor, County Auditor, State Board of Equalization and the County Board of Equalization as to the assessment of the net profits of mines, the statements and returns to be made, the equalization thereof and other official acts, are the same as those provided by the laws of this State for the assessment of other property. (Section 6 of Act of February 17, 1903.)

Sec. 41. If any person, corporation or association engaged in mining as mentioned in this act, refuses or neglects to make and deliver to the assessor of the county where the mines are located, the statement mentioned in this act, such assessor must list the property and assess according to his knowledge and information, the amount of said tax in the manner provided by the law for the assessment of other property, where no statement is furnished. (Section 7 of Act of February 17, 1903.)

Sec. 42. The assessor after such statement has been rendered shall have the right to examine the books and accounts of any person, corporation or association engaged in mining as mentioned in this chapter in order to verify the statement made by such person, corporation or association, and if from such examination he finds such statement false, he must assess the net proceeds in the same manner as if no statement had been made and delivered, by making an estimate from the best sources within his reach, and if satisfied that the false statement was intentionally so made he shall add as a penalty therefor, to the amount of the net proceeds so found, by 50 per cent. thereof which amount thus increased shall constitute the sum upon which the taxes must be levied and collected, and such assessment shall be binding, effectual and lawful and the value so fixed by the assessor shall not be reduced by the County Board of Equalization.

. All information derived from any examination of the books and accounts made pursuant to this act by the assessor, or any one acting for him or representing him, shall be deemed to be and held as confidential communications not to be communicated to any other person by the person making such examination, or any one to whom the knowledge of such examination or facts therein disclosed shall come, except that it becomes necessary as a part of the performance of the public duty of such person to disclose the same in any proceeding affecting the validity of said assessment or taxation or for the prosecution for perjury of the person required to make the statement mentioned in this act. And any person or officer making such disclosure or violating such confidence, except as herein provided, shall be deemed guilty of a felony and upon conviction thereof shall be removed from office and punished as in case of other felonies.

Nothing in this act contained must be construed so as to exempt from taxation, improvements, buildings, erections, structures or machinery placed upon any mining claim or used in connection therewith. (Section 8 of Act of February 17, 1903.)

Sec. 43. The tax mentioned in the preceding sections must be collected and payment thereof enforced as the collection and enforcement of other taxes are provided for, and every such tax is a lien upon the mine or mining claim from which the ores or minerals are extracted, which lien attaches on the second Monday of January of each year, and the sale thereof for delinquent taxes may be made as provided for the sale of real estate for delinquent taxes. (Section 9 of Act of February 17, 1903.)

Sec. 44. If any one herein required to make a statement, shall knowingly and willfully swear to any false statement contained therein, then such person shall be guilty of perjury and shall be prosecuted and punished as provided for in other cases of perjury. (Section 10 of Act of February 17, 1903.)

Sec. 45. All acts and parts of acts in conflict herewith or inconsistent with this act are hereby repealed. (Section 11 of Act of February 17, 1903.)

Sec. 46. Whereas an emergency exists therefor, this act shall take effect immediately from and after its passage. (Section 12 of Act of February 17, 1903.)

Act of Idaho State Legislature of February 17, 1903.

## MINERS' LIENS.

Sec. 47. Every person performing labor upon or furnishing materials to be used in the construction, alteration or repair of any mining claim, building, wharf, bridge, ditch, dike, flume, tunnel, fence, machinery, railroad, wagon road, acqueduct to create hydraulic power or any other structure, or who performs labor in any mine or mining claim, has a lien upon the same for work or labor done or materials furnished, whether done or furnished at the instance of the owner of the building or other improvement or his agent; and every contractor, sub-contractor, architect, builder or any person having charge of any mining or of the construction, alteration or repair either in whole or in part, of any building or other improvement, as aforesaid shall be held to be the agent of and owner for the purpose of this chapter: Provided, That the lessee or lessees of any mining claim shall not be considered as the agent or agents of the owner under the provisions of this chapter. (Section 1 of Act of February 7, 1899.)

## MINERS' CUSTOMS AND RULES.

Sec. 48. In actions respecting mining claims, proof must be admitted of the customs, usuages, or regulations established and in force at the bar or diggings, embracing such claim and such customs, usages or regulations when not in conflict with the laws of this State, must govern the decision of the action.   (Section 4547, Revised Statutes of Idaho.)

### MINERS MAY DEVELOP MINES ON SQUATTERS' CLAIMS.

Sec. 49.   Any person being a citizen of the United States, or having in accordance with the law declared his intention to become a citizen, occupying and settled upon, any of the public lands of the United States in this State, for the purpose of cultivating or grazing the same, may commence and maintain any action for interference with, or injury to his possession of such land against any person interfering with or injuring the same; but if such land contains mines of any of the precious metals, the possession or claim of the person occupying the same for the purposes aforesaid must not prevent the working of such mines by persons desiring to work the same, as fully as if no such claim for agricultural or grazing purposes had been made thereon:   Provided, That this chapter must not be so construed as to allow a person, subsequent to the location of land for agricultural or grazing purposes to go upon such lands for the purpose of mining without first paying the owner thereof the value of any growing crops they may destroy; this provision does not extend to any crops planted subsequent to their location for mining purposes; and this chapter must not be construed to authorize the maintenance of any claim upon lands which at the commencement of any such action, may have been selected by the United States, and reserved for any purpose.   (Section 4552, Revised Statutes of Idaho.)

### WHO MAY TAKE HOLD OF AND DISPOSE OF MINING PROPERTY.

Sec. 50.   Any person whether citizen or alien (except as hereinafter provided) natural or artificial, may take, hold and dispose of mining claims and mining property, real or personal, tunnel rights, mill sites, quartz mills and reduction works used or necessary or proper for the reduction of ores, and water rights used for mining or milling purposes, and any other lands or property necessary for the working of mines or the reduction of the products thereof:   Provided, That Chinese or persons of Mongolian descent not born in the United States, are not permitted to acquire title to land or any real property under the provisions of this title.   (Section 1 of Act of March 2, 1891.)

### MINE INSPECTOR.

Sec. 51.   It shall be the duty of the Inspector of Mines, at least once each year, to visit in person each mining county in the State of Idaho and examine all such mines therein, as in his judgment, may require examination for the purpose of determining the condition of such mines as to safety, and to collect information and statistics relative to mines and mining and the mineral resources of the State, and to collect, arrange and classify mineral and geological specimens found in this State and to forward the same to the State School of Mines. (Section 4 of Act of February 14, 1899.)

Sec. 52.   Said Inspector shall have full power and authority, at all reasonable hours, to enter and examine any and all mines in this State, and shall have the right to enter into any and all mine stopes, levels, winzes, tunnels, shafts, drifts, cross-cuts, workings and machinery, for the purpose of such examination; and the owner, lessor, lessee, agent, manager or other person in charge of such mine or mines, shall render the Inspector such assistance as may be required by the

Inspector to enable him to make a full, thorough and complete examination of each and every part of such mine or mines, and whenever, as a result of the examination of any mine, (whether such examination is made in consequence of a complaint, as hereinafter provided, or otherwise), the Inspector shall find the same to be in an unsafe condition, he shall at once serve, or cause to be served, a written notice upon the owner, lessor, lessee, agent, manager or other person in charge of such mine, stating in detail in what particular or particulars the mine is dangerous or insecure, and shall require all necessary changes to be made, without delay, for the purpose of making said mine safe for the employees therein. Upon the neglect or refusal of any owner, lessor, lessee, agent, manager or other person in charge, so notified to comply with the requirements stated in such notice so served, such owner, lessor, lessee, agent, manager or other person in charge of such mine, shall be deemed guilty of a misdemeanor, and is punishable by a fine of not more than five hundred dollars, and each day's continuance of such neglect or refusal shall be a separate offense, and in case of any criminal or civil proceeding at law against the party or parties so notified, on account of the loss of life or bodily injury sustained by any employee subsequent to the service of such notice, and in consequence of a neglect or refusal to obey the Inspector's requirement, a certified copy of the notice served by the Inspector shall be prima facie evidence of the culpable negligence of the party or parties so notified. (Section 5 of the Act of February 14, 1899.)

Sec. 53. It is hereby made the duty of the owner, lessor, lessee, agent, manager or other person in charge of each and every mine, of whatever kind or character, within the State, to forward to the Inspector of Mines, at his office, not later than the first day of June in each year, a detailed report showing the character of the mine, the number of men then employed, and the estimated maximum number of men to be employed therein during the ensuing year, the method of working such mine, and the general condition thereof, and such owner, lessor, lessee, agent, manager or other person in charge of any mine, within the state, must furnish whatever information relative to such mine as the Inspector of Mines may, from time to time require, for his guidance in the proper discharge of his official duties. (Part of Section 6 of Act of February 14, 1899.)

Sec. 54. Whenever the Inspector of Mines shall receive a formal complaint in writing, signed by three or more persons, setting forth that the mine in which they are employed is dangerous in any respect, he shall, in person, visit and examine such mine: Provided, Every such formal complaint shall in all cases specifically set forth the nature of the danger existing at the mine and shall describe with as much certainty as is possible, how much danger, apparent or real, renders such mine dangerous, and shall set forth the time when such danger was first observed, and shall distinctly set forth whether, or not, any notice of such defect or danger has been given by the complainants or any one else to their knowledge, to the superintendent or other person in charge of such mine, and if no such complaint has been made to such superintendent or other person in charge the reason why it has not been made: and Provided Further, That all complaints shall be duly verified by the parties complaining, before some officer authorized by law to administer oaths. After such complaint shall have received by the Inspector of Mines, it shall be the duty of such Inspector to serve a certified copy thereof, but without the names of the complainants, upon the owner, lessor, lessee, agent, manager or other person in charge, and as soon as possible after receiving such complaint to visit and examine such mine, and if from such examination he shall find such complaint to be just, he shall give notice in writing of the danger existing to the owner, lessor, lessee, agent, manager or other person in charge thereof, and in such notice may, at his discretion, order such mine or workings in which such danger exists, closed until such danger has been removed. The names of the complainants complaining as in this section provided, shall not, under any circumstances, be divulged to any person by said Inspector except such action be necessary in the administration of justice in the courts of the State. (Section 7 of Act of February 14. 1899.)

Sec. 55. And it shall be the duty of the Inspector of Mines, upon the neglect or refusal of any owner, lessor, lessee, agent, manager, or other person, in charge of any mine or working, notified of the unsafe or dangerous condition of his mine, promptly to comply with the requirements of the notice served upon him, to at once notify the Attorney-General of such neglect or refusal, and the Attorney-General, must thereupon immediately commence action in the name of the State against the party so notified for the recovery of the penalty mentioned in Section 5, in any court of competent jurisdiction, and the amount so recovered shall be paid into the general school fund of the State, and constitute a part thereof. (Section 8 of the Act of February 14, 1899.)

Sec. 56. Whenever a serious or fatal accident shall occur in any mine in the State of Idaho, it shall be the duty of the owner, lessor. lessee, agent, manager or other person in charge thereof, immediately. and by the quickest means, to notify the Inspector of Mines or his deputy as may be most convenient, of such accident; and upon receiving such notice the Inspector or his deputy, or both, shall at once repair to the place of the accident and investigate fully the cause of such accident; and the Inspector or his deputy shall be present at any coroner's inquest held over the remains of any person or persons killed in any such accident, and shall have power at such inquest to examine and cross-examine witnesses, and may have process to compel the attendance of necessary witnesses at such inquest. If the Inspector or deputy inspector cannot be immediately present in case of a fatal or serious accident occurring, it shall be the duty of the owner, lessor, lessee, agent, manager or other person in charge of the mine in which such accident has occurred, to have statements made and verified by those witnessing such accident; in case of no person being present at the time of the accident, then the statement of those first present thereafter shall be taken, which statement shall be verified. and such verified statements shall be placed in the hands of the Inspector or deputy inspector, upon the demand of such officer. Whenever any deputy inspector is present at any coroner's inquest and assists in the examination, he shall at the conclusion thereof at once prepare and forward to the Inspector a full and detailed report of the accident, giving all information obtainable regarding the same. (Section 10 of Act of February 14, 1899.)

We have now given the law relating to mines and mining, both United States (in the first chapter) and State of Idaho, (in the present one), or so much thereof as is of special interest to the prospector and miner. The acquisition and possession of all mining properties located in the future will be governed by the provisions and regulations of the laws as given, until changes shall be made therein by Congress or the Idaho State Legislature.

To emphasize the necessity of complying with the requirements of the Statutes already given in seeking to secure their benefits and possess and work mineral claims, the full text of the case of Brown et al. vs. Levan et al. is herein given. The syllabus, statement and decision gives fully the facts in the case, and law governing the same.

### SUPREME COURT OF IDAHO, June 1, 1896.

#### Brown et al. vs. Levan et al.

1. In locating mining claims it has become the settled law that Section 2324 of the United States Revised Statutes must be complied with.

2. That the record must contain such a description of the claim by reference to some natural object or permanent monument as will identify the claim.

3. Such reference to a natural object or permanent monument must be such as to furnish a reasonable certainty that the locus of the claim has not been and could not well be changed.

4. Permanent monuments may be erected for the purpose of tying the claim to them, but then courses and distances from them to discovery stake or corner stakes or some object on the ground must be stated with reasonable accuracy. (Syllabus by the Court.)

In the trial of this action in the District Court, Boise County, plaintiffs John Brown and others were non-suited, from that judgment they appealed.

In this case the plaintiffs allege that they were and are the owners of and in possession of the Magpie mining claim on the North side of Willow Creek, in Boise County, Idaho, in what was then an unorganized district, now known as "West View Mining District." The claim was located September 10, 1892, by John Brown. William Francis wrote the notice of the location for plaintiff. The Magpie and two other claims, named the "Kid" and "Greyhound" were recorded on the same day, but it appears from the evidence that the two latter claims were located after the Magpie. Brown, the plaintiff, testified that he took the notice off of the discovery stake of the Magpie and took it to Boise City, to T. J. Curtis. The latter copied it and Brown took the copy thus written to the Recorder and had it recorded in the Recorder's Office of Ada County. It was afterwards discovered that the ground located was in Boise County. Then the same notice was taken to the Recorder's Office in Boise County, and there recorded. The original notice was taken back and placed on the stake as before. It remained there for some time and was finally washed off. Brown, the plaintiff and locator, states that he worked nearly two months on the claim in 1892; 60 or 61 days in 1893; that he went to the claim in 1894, some time in August and found the defendant, Levan, there with his men. Brown and Levan had a dispute over the claim at that time. The stakes that had been erected as shown by the evidence of Brown and others were then down and removed from the claim, and the discovery shaft, as plaintiff described it, "was filled up just about natural, and the claim showed no work anywhere." Brown stated further that Francis wrote the notice for him. That he himself, not being able to write does not know what was in the notice. A copy of the notice was introduced in evidence, which was in part as follows

The mining claim hereby located is situated in..........Mining
District. Boise County. State of Idaho, and is more particularly described as follows to-wit:    Being situated and located on the North
side of North Willow Creek about one-half mile from the Hurt mines,
the direction being southwest.    The adjoining claims are the "Gem of
the Woods" claim on the North and the "Kid" claim on the South
and the "Greyhound" on the East.    This location is distinctly marked
on the ground, so that its boundaries can be readily traced by a stake
set at discovery shaft where this notice and statement is posted, this
10th day of September, 1892, and by substantial posts or monuments
of stone at each corner of the claim, and exterior boundaries of the
claim as marked by said posts or monuments are as follows, to-wit:

Beginning at discovery and running thence in a northerly direction
three hundred feet to a stake; thence in a westerly direction fifteen
hundred feet, to a monument; thence in a southerly direction, six
hundred feet to a stake; thence in an easterly direction fifteen hundred feet, to a stake; thence in a northerly direction three hundred
feet to the place of beginning—including all surface ground within
said boundaries.

The undersigned intend to hold their claim under and according to
the laws of the United States and of the State of Idaho, and to record
this notice and statement under oath in the County Recorder's Office
of said County. as provided by law. ,

Dated this tenth day of September, 1892.

(Signed.)                                        JOHN BROWN.
                                                  JOHN RANSOM,
                                                  Locator and Claimant.

Evidence was also  introduced as to the manner in which the
boundaries of the claims were marked on the ground, and also testimony to show what was known as the Hurt mines; and where they
were situated.    Much other testimony was introduced, some of which
will be referred to hereafter.    The plaintiff then rested, and the defendant moved a non-suit which was allowed by the Court.    After stating the facts, the opinion of the Court was thus rendered by Chief
Justice Morgan.

The specifications of error are as follows:    First, The Court erred
in granting the motion for and entering judgment of non-suit; Second,
The Court erred in refusing to admit the evidence of Hastings as to
the value of the ore extracted from the Magpie claim by defendants,
based upon samples taken by witnesses from the veins surrounding
the ore that had been extracted.    The ground upon which the motion
for non-suit was made and sustained is:    Because said location notice
fails to designate either natural objects or permanent monuments, as
required by the Revised Statutes of the United States, (Section 2324)
so that the location of the claim could be accurately determined;
and because said notice does not contain a description of the locality
of the claim by reference to natural land marks or fixed objects and
contiguous claims, so as to render the situation or locality of the
claim reasonably certain as required by Section 3102, Revised Statutes
of Idaho.

Section 2324, Revised Statutes of the United States, requires that
all records of mining claims shall contain, such a description of the
claim or claims located by reference to some natural object or permanent monument as will identify the claim.

In the case of Drummond vs. Long, 9 Colo., 538, the location notice, after describing the boundaries of the claim, states further: "The discovery shaft being situated upon said lode, within the lines of said claim in Uncompaghree Mining District, County of LaPlata, Territory of Colorado, on the southwest side of Mt. Hardon, in Portland Gulch, about 1500 feet north of the Hawkeye Lode." With reference to this location, the Court says: "In the certificate before us we do not find any such reference to either a natural object or permanent monument as meets the substantial requirements of the statute. Describing the lode as being on the southwest side of Mt. Hardon and in Portland Gulch, locates the lode generally. It is not, however, that definite location by reference that the statute contemplates." Citing Faxon vs. Barnard, 4 Fed., 702: "The certificate also describes the discovery shaft of the Portland as being about 1500 feet north of the Hawkeye Lode. We assume, however, that it has been duly located in compliance with the laws of Congress and of the State; that it is in the usual form of a parallelogram 1500 feet in length, by 300 feet in width; and that it contains about 10 acres. A tract of land of such dimensions cannot be treated either as a natural object or permanent monument within the meaning of the act of Congress. The discovery shaft of the Portland it not tied definitely to any corner or monument of either the location or lode. From what point on the Hawkeye location or lode is one to start to find and identify the discovery shaft of the Portland? With a starting point anywhere in a parallelogram of ten acres, the discovery shaft is anywhere by 1500 feet distant in ten acres to the north. Under such conditions identification with that reasonable certainty required by the statute is an impossibility; and it cannot be said that the statute in this respect has been complied with. To hold otherwise would leave the requirement of but little practical utility. The insufficiency of the location certificate is apparent upon its face, and we do not see that it can be aided by evidence aliunde. The effect of the omission is to leave the certificate of the location void." Citing Mining Co. vs. Drake, 8 Colo., 586. In Gleason vs. Mining Co., 13 Nev., 462, the Court says: "The object of the law in requiring the location to be marked on the ground is to fix the claim, to prevent floating or swinging, so that those who in good faith are looking for unoccupied claims in the vicinity of previous locations may be enabled to ascertain exactly what has been appropriated in order to make their locations upon the residue. We concede that the provisions of the law designed for the retainment of this object are most important and beneficient, and they ought not be frittered away by construction." In Faxon vs. Barnard, Fed., 704, the Court says: "The description of the location of the mining claim is as follows: Situate on the north side of Iowa Gulch, about timberline, on the west side of Bald Mt. said claim is staked and marked as the law directs." Of this the Court says: "It is utterly impossible to find in this language any reference to a natural object or permanent monument defining the location, and the only question is as to the effect of the omission. The act of Congress requires such reference to be made in the description of a claim, and the State Legislature has declared that a certificate shall give such description as shall identify the claim with reasonable certainty." In Mining Co. vs. Drake, supra, the description was as follows: "Beginning at the westerly end of the Gilpin County Mining Company's property on the Williams lode in Lake Gulch Mining District, running thence in a westerly direction a distance of 50 feet to the easterly end of Packard and Updegraph's property on said lode." Of this description the Court says: "It is conceded that the claims referred to are patented claims, and they may supply the permanent monuments required by the act of Congress. Still the reference thereto in the location certificate, and the description of the claim located, are too indefinite to enable the same to be fully identified, or its boundaries readily traced from this certificate alone. Beginning at the westerly end of a certain mining claim. At what point of the westerly end? Was it at the corner, or in the center or some other point on the line of this westerly end? The certificate does not tell. Running thence in a westerly direction a distance of fifty feet to the easterly end of Packard and Updegraft's property on said lode. What part of the easterly end of this property did this line intersect? Where was the discovery shaft situated with reference to this line? To what fixed point is said shaft or any other part of said claim tied? It is apparent that no information is furnished by this certificate which will enable any one to trace the boundaries of this claim. The discovery shaft is tied to nothing definitely, nor is any corner or point of the claim, so far as appears from this record. The statute pronounces such a location certificate void. There was therefore no error in rejecting it." In Darger vs. Le Sieur (Utah) the location notice was as follows: "This is to certify that, we, the undersigned have this day located and claim 1500 feet in length on this ledge of shale and wax and 300 feet on each side of the center of location. We claim 300 feet running east and 1200 feet running west from the monument. This ledge is situated up near the head of the right hand fork of what is known as 'Tie Canyon' about five miles from the D. & R. G. R. R. in Utah County," etc. With reference to this notice, the Court says: "We think the Court erred in admitting in evidence, plaintiff's location notices. They are fatally defective, and valid locations cannot be made under them. The Revised Statutes of the United States require that there must be such a description of the claim located by reference to some natural object or permanent monument, as will identify it. Assuming that the D. & R. G. R. R. had a track in Utah County, an officer armed with a writ of restitution under the verdict and judgment could not, from the description given, put plaintiffs in possession of their claims. They are described as being about five miles from the railroad track, but in what direction or from what point on the railroad track is not stated." In Drummond vs. Long, 9 Colo., 560, the Court says, with reference to what may be designated as a permanent monument: "The intention of the provision is to give one seeking the locus of a recorded claim something in the nature of an initial point from which to start, and following the course or distance given, find with reasonable certainty the claim located. The identification must be by reference to some natural object or permanent monument. Stone monuments, blazed trees, the confluence of streams, the point of intersection of some well known gulches, ravines or roads, permanent buttes, hills, mining shafts, etc., are enumerated as satisfying the requirements of the law. In the certificate before us we do not find any such reference to either a natural object or permanent monument as meets the substantial requirements of the statute." In Dillion vs. Bayless, (Mont.), the Court says: "We are prepared to concede that no matter how permanent and prominent the monument may be or how conspicuous and certain the natural object is, yet, if there was no intelligent reference to them that would identify the claim, the description would not satisfy the requirements of the United States law. The very object of selecting a natural object or erecting or referring to a permanent monument is in the language of the statute, to identify the claim."

Judge Hallet, in Faxon vs. Barnard, supra, says: The Government gives its lands to those citizens who may discover precious metal ores therein, upon the condition that they will define the subject of the grant with such certainty as may be necessary to prevent mistakes on the part of the Government and on the part of other citizens who may be asking the same bounty. This is reasonable and necessary to justly administer the law and therefore it must be said that without such description a certificate of location is void." See also Darger vs. LeSieur, supra. To the same effect we might cite many other cases if it were necessary.

From these authorities it is evident that it has become the settled law of the land that Section 2324, Revised Statutes of United States, must be complied with, to-wit: That all records of mining claims shall contain such a description of the claim or claims located by reference to some natural object or permanent monument as will identify the claim. The location notice of the Magpie described the mine as located on the north side of North Willow Creek. This portion of the reference is, of course, so indefinite and uncertain that it amounts to no reference at all when taken alone. It is indefinite as the reference of the Mary Bell lode in Darger vs. LeSieur, supra, which describes the claim as situated about five miles from the D. & R. G. R. R. track, near the head of the right hand fork of what is known as Tie Canyon. Concerning this notice of location and five others of the same tenor, the Court in the above case says that they are fatally defective, and valid locations cannot be made upon them. Putting the whole reference together, which of course is proper and is it any better? Namely, "Situated on the North Side of North Willow Creek, about one-half mile from the Hurt mines, the direction being southwest; the Gem of the Woods claim on the North, and the Kid Claim on the South and Greyhound on the East." Concerning the Hurt mines, Bradford Hurt, the son of the first locator, testifies: "We (that is Bradford Hurt, and his father), were interested in four claims. They were the Birthday, the Old Man, Gray Eagle, and the Silver Leaf. The mines which are known as the Hurt mines, are the Birthday, Old Man, Gray Eagle and Silver Leaf. The Silver Leaf is southeast of the Magpie; joins, or nearly joins it. The Old Man is east of the Magpie. The Gray Eagle is east of the Old Man, and the Birthday is northeast of the Old Man. These claims do not all join; they do not connect exactly. The Silver Leaf does not join the rest. The other three joined at that time. The Old Man is not 1000 feet from the Magpie. It possibly may be 1000 feet. It is six or eight hundred." William Francis testifies: "I know about the Hurt mines— The Birthday, Old Man mine, and the Silver Spray. There are a number of mines over there known as the Hurt mines. The Silver Spray is southwest of the Magpie, the Old Man is 1000 feet east of the Magpie." John Brown, the plaintiff, testifies: "Hurt has three mines on North Willow Creek, I believe—the Silver Leaf, the Old Man and the Birthday. Some call the Birthday, the 'Hurt mine,' and some call the Old Man the 'Hurt mine.' Mr. Hurt has three mines over there. I believe. Hurt has an interest in the Silver Leaf and some call it the 'Hurt mine' because he is in it." No attempt was made to show that there was any mistake made in writing the location notice and we must take it as we find it, and must presume that the intention was, as stated in the notice, to refer to the Hurt mines as a permanent monument by which to identify and from which to determine the location of the Magpie. Now if we make a diagram of the Hurt mines, and place them in any position that will correspond with the testimony, then draw a line from the Northwest to the Southeast, about one-half mile to the Southwest of the Hurt mines, we shall see at once that half a dozen mines may be located, and each one in a southwesterly direction from the Hurt mines, and all north of North Willow Creek. It is not at all surprising that Mr. Hastings, the surveyor, at first said he could not find the mine from the location notice, and then, partially taking it back, says that he did not try to. There was no discovery shaft or cut on the ground when Mr. Hastings went there to survey the claim, nothing to indicate that any work had ever been done. The discovery stake might have been moved many times, and no one unacquainted with the location could have discovered from the location notice that it has been so moved. We think it is the duty of the Court to give mining notices and records a liberal construction, to the end of upholding a location made in good faith. But where the description and reference to a natural object or permanent monument is of such a character that a mining engineer could not find the claim from the location notice, as is evident in the case, and where it is such that the claim may be floated almost anywhere to suit the ground or to cover ore that may have been since discovered, it is clearly such a notice as cannot furnish a foundation for a valid location. It appears, from Mr. Hastings' testimony that he placed the discovery at the point indicated in his testimony, not from any direction in the location notice, nor on account of any indications on the ground that any work had been done, but from statements made by plaintiff; and hence all his measurements, being made from an uncertain point, were themselves uncertain, and the Court is unable to say whether this was the original location or not. We may presume that plaintiff Brown was perfectly honest in pointing out the place of discovery, and the corners of the claim, as the evidence shows he did so point out the corners to the surveyor; but where there is such uncertainty in the location notice we have no certainty of it at all. It is evident that the reference to some natural object or permanent monument to identify the claim must be such as to furnish a reasonable certainty that the locus of the claim has not been and could not well be changed. The naming of contiguous claims is a requirement of our statute and was complied with, but the reference to a permanent monument must be such as will enable a skilled engineer, at least, to identify the claim, without reference to contiguous claims the location of which is uncertain. Permanent monuments may exist before the location, or may be erected for the purpose of tying the claim to them; but then courses and distances from them to discovery stake or corner stakes or some other object on the ground must be stated with reasonable accuracy.

The judgment of the Court below is affirmed. Sullivan and Houston, J. J., concur.

A study of above case shows how strictly the law insists on a compliance with the pre-requisites of a valid location, illustrating that one of tying the claim to some natural object or permanent monument as provided in the United States statute. Other cases might be cited showing the necessity of strictly complying with the other essentials, to a valid location, such as a discovery in place and annual labor, etc., subsequently, however, to the rendering of the foregoing decision and under date of February 4, 1902, the Supreme Court of Idaho in the case of Morrison et al. vs. Regan rendered a decision somewhat modifying the foregoing decision in some respects and placing · less rigid construction on the law requiring the tying of the claim to a natural object or permanent monument.

## SUPREME COURT OF IDAHO, February 4, 1902.
### Morrison et al. vs. Regan.

### Mining Claim—Location—Certificate—Rejection—Notice—Amendment—Evidence.

Sullivan, J.—This is an action in support of an adverse claim made by the plaintiff against the application for a patent made by the defendant to the Summit Lode mining Claim, situated in French Mining District, Owyhee County. The complaint alleges, inter alia, that the plaintiffs were the owners of a certain lode mining claim known as the Bullion; that said claim was located on the 1st day of January, 1887, by James Shaw and Simon Morrison; that on the 19th day of September, 1900, the plaintiffs by their agent made an amended location of said Bullion claim; that the plaintiffs and their grantors have performed the annual work required by law upon said Bullion claim from the date of its location to the present time, and have performed all other acts required to entitle them to hold said claim, and that during all the time since January 1, 1887, the plaintiffs and their grantors have been in the actual, open, notorious, undisputed and uninterrupted possession of said premises; that on the 10th day of January, 1901, the defendant filed in the United States Land Office, at Boise City, an application for a patent to the Summit lode mining claim, which conflicts with and overlaps the said Bullion claim. The answer denies the validity of the Bullion location, and puts in issue the material allegations of the complaint. A cross complaint was filed by the defendant, which was answered by the plaintiffs. On the trial plaintiffs introduced some evidence of discovery, location posting and recording of notice of location, and thereupon offered in evidence the location notice, which is as follows:

"Bullion. Notice of Relocation. Notice is hereby given that we, the undersigned, having complied with the requirements of Chapter 6 of Title Thirty-two of the Revised Statutes of the United States, and of the laws of Idaho Territory, relating to the location of mining claims, and all local customs, laws and regulations, have located six hundred (600) linear feet along this lode or vein of quartz, by three hundred (300) feet on each side of the middle of the vein or lode, making 600 feet in width. This claim so located is hereby named the Bullion Mine, and is situated in French Mining District, Owyhee County, Idaho Territory, and is described as follows: Commencing at this stake and notice, which is situated about 300 feet in a northwesterly direction from the Minnesota mine—this is an extension of the Red Jacket mine—and running thence along the vein or lode in a southerly direction to similar stake and notice. We, the undersigned, claim six hundred (600) linear feet in a southerly direction from this stake and notice to a similar stake and notice. This claim is six hundred (600) linear feet long. Dated January 1st, year 1887. Locators:

James Shaw, 300 feet.  Simon Morrison 300 feet.

Territory of Idaho,      } ss.
County of Owyhee,

I, James Shaw, do solemnly swear that I am acquainted with the mining ground described in the notice of location herewith called the Bullion ledge, lode or claim, and that the ground and claim therein described, or any part thereof, has not, to the best of my knowledge and belief, been heretofore located according to the laws of the United States and of this Territory, or if so located, that the same has been abandoned or forfeited by reason of the failure of such former locators to comply in respect thereto, with the requirements of said laws.

JAMES SHAW.

Subscribed and sworn to before me this first day of January, 1887.

JAMES LYMAN, County Recorder.

Filed January 1, 1887, at 2 o'clock p. m.

JAMES LYMAN, County Recorder.

Recorded in Book 7 of Mining claims, on pages 260 and 261, among the records of Owyhee County, Idaho. (Certified by E. L. Ballard, ex-officio Recorder of said Owyhee County, to be a correct copy of the original record.)

Counsel for defendant objected to the introduction of said notice on the ground that there is no such description in the notice, by reference to such natural objects or permanent land marks or contiguous claims as is sufficient to identify the claim under the statutes. Thereupon James Shaw was called as a witness and testified that the Minnesota and Red Jacket mines mentioned in said notice were well known claims and that as near as he could recollect, the Minnesota claim was 600 feet by 100 feet, after which said objection was argued by respective counsel. The objection was sustained by the Court, and the notice of location was not admitted in evidence.

George A. Sonneman was then called by plaintiffs, and testified that he made an amended location of said Bullion lode by authority of the owners; that he had a lease and bond on the same, and that thereunder he had the right to work said Bullion lode and also had the privileges of perfecting the title and applying for a patent; that he made an amended location of said Bullion lode on the 19th day of September, 1900; thereupon said amended location notice was offered in evidence, which offer was objected to by counsel for the defendant for the reasons that a void original location notice is not susceptible of amendment; that the testimony does not show the person who made the amended location had proper authority to make it; that the pleadings show that between the date of the original location and date of the amended location, in 1900, rights to claims upon which the defendant is applying for patent have intervened and for the reason that no amended location can be made so as to cut off intervening rights, and that the amended location is not in the names of the same parties that made the original location. In passing upon that objection, the trial Court said, "I am inclined to think that this amended location becomes effective only by reason of the fact that there was an original location. The Court has held that there was no original location-so far as the evidence in this case is concerned and that being true, there was nothing to amend." The objection was then sustained and the Court refused to admit said amended location notice in evidence. Thereupon the witness, James Shaw, was recalled and testified that the lode claim for which the defendant is applying for a patent was located January 1, 1892, five years after the location of said Bullion claim; that he had done the assessment work annually on the Bullion since its location in 1887. Counsel for plaintiffs then offered in evidence certified copies of proof of labor on said Bullion claim, which offer was objected to on the ground that proof of labor was entirely immaterial, for the reason that the Court had excluded the original notice of location, and had held that void. The objection was sustained by the Court. Thereafter counsel for plaintiffs offered other evidence in support of the allegations of the complaint and under the objection of counsel for the defendant, it was all rejected on the ground that it was immaterial, for the reason that the original location notice had been excluded and declared void, and for that reason no further questions were proper. Thereafter on motion of counsel for defendant, the cross complaint was dismissed. Thereafter counsel for plaintiffs asked permission to recall the notice that they had rested their case, and asked permission to introduce proofs of the present ownership of said Bullion lode mining claim, to which request counsel for defendant objected, on the ground that the Court had already excluded the location notice of said Bullion claim, and for that reason the question of ownership was not before the Court, which objection was sustained by the Court. Counsel for defendant then moved for a non-suit on the ground that plaintiffs had failed to prove any valid location of the Bullion lode mining claim, or any right, title or interest to the ground in conflict; that plaintiffs take nothing by his action; and that the same be dismissed, without costs against the plaintiffs. The motion was granted, and judgment of non-suit was entered. This appeal is from the judgment.

Twelve errors are assigned on which the plaintiffs, who are appellants, rely for a reversal of the judgment. The refusal of the Court to admit in evidence the original location notice of the Bullion mining claim is assigned as error, a copy of which notice is above set forth. When said notice was offered in evidence counsel for the respondent objected to its introduction on the ground that it contained no such description, by reference to such natural objects or permanent landmarks or contiguous claims, sufficient to identify said claim, as required by law. After said offer and objection was made and before a ruling thereon, by the Court, counsel for appellants, by the witness, James Shaw, proved that the Minnesota and Red Jacket mines named in said notice of location were well known claims, and that the Minnesota claim was 600 by 100 feet. The objection was then argued and submitted to the Court for decision. The objection was sustained and the notice excluded.

It is contended that said notice of location failed to comply with the provisions of Section 2324, Revised Statutes of the United States, and Section 3102, Revised Statutes of Idaho. Section 2324, Revised Statutes of the United States is as follows: "All records of mining claims hereafter made shall contain the names of the locators, the date of the location, and such description of the claim or claims located by reference to some natural object or permanent monuments as will identify the claim." Section 3102, Revised Statutes of Idaho, is as follows: "The notice must contain the date of the location, the names of the locators, the name of the claim, ledge or lode, the quantity in feet claimed along the ledge or lode, the width claimed from the middle of the vein and must also give such a description of the locality of the claim, by reference to natural landmarks or fixed objects, and contiguous claims, if there be any, as to render the situation of the same reasonably certain from the letter of the notice itself."

The Court held that the location notice of the Bullion claim did not sufficiently comply with the provisions of said sections of the Revised Statutes of the United States and of the State of Idaho, above quoted and refused to permit its introduction as evidence. That ruling of the Court was based on the decisions of this Court in Brown vs. Levan (Idaho), 46 Pac., 661, and Railroad Co. vs. San Garde (Idaho), 61, Pac., 137. And because of the meager statement of the facts in the case of Brown vs. Levan we are not surprised that the Court held the Bullion lode notice of location defective, in that it failed, to "give such a description of the locality of the claim, by reference to natural landmarks or fixed objects and contiguous claims, as to render the situation of the same reasonably certain from the letter of the notice itself." That case involved the title to the Magpie mining claim, and that portion of the location notice purporting to comply with the provisions of the sections of statute above quoted is as follows: "The mining claim hereby located is situated in.............. Mining District, Boise County, State of Idaho, and is particularly described as follows, to-wit: Being situated and located on the north side of North Willow Creek, about one-half mile from the Hurt mines, the direction being southwest. The adjoining claims are the Gem of the Woods on the north, the Kid on the south and the Greyhound on the east." On the trial of said cause, in support of the allegations of the complaint, and to show the location of said Magpie claim, said notice of location was introduced, also oral testimony as to what was known as the "Hurt mines" mentioned in said notice and it also appeared that neither the Kid mining claim nor the Greyhound mining claim, referred to in said location notice as adjoining claims, were located at the time of the location of the Magpie and that the Gem of the Woods claim, therein mentioned never was located and as neither of said mentioned claims had been located when the Magpie location was made, reference to them as natural landmarks or fixed objects or as contiguous claims could not be made a compliance with said provisions of the Statutes of Idaho and the United States supra. The evidence as to what constituted the "Hurt mines" as referred to in said location notice, is largely quoted in said opinion and it is not necessary to quote it here. It is sufficient to say, that the evidence clearly showed that there were no "Hurt mines" located about one-half mile in a southeasterly direction from the Magpie. William Francis testified that the Silver Spray mine, one of the "Hurt mines," was located southwest of the Magpie, and the Old Man mine, which was another Hurt mine, was located about 1000 feet east of the Magpie. Hurt testified that the Silver Leaf, another of the Hurt claims, was southeast of the Magpie, and joins or nearly joins it, that the Old Man is east of the Magpie and the Grey Eagle east of the Old Man claim. The evidence entirely fails to show that the Hurt mines were about one-half mile northeast of the Magpie claim or that the Magpie claim is about one-half mile southwest of the Hurt mines. One of the Hurt mines was southwest of the Magpie, and another adjoining the Magpie, or nearly so on the east and another about 1000 feet east of it, and the Birthday claim about a half a mile northeast of it. Under those facts the Court held that the reference in said notice of location to the Hurt mines as a permanent monument was not a sufficient compliance with the provisions o. the above quoted statutes.

The evidence clearly showed the mines known as the "Hurt mines," in that locality were not about one-half a mile in a northeasterly direction from the Magpie claim and contiguous. One claim was southwest of it, another east of it and adjoining it, and another about 1000 feet east of it and another about one-half mile northeast of it. Said four claims were known as the "Hurt mines." Being so scattered and in divers directions from the Magpie claim they were not a natural landmark or fixed object such as would identify the Magpie claim by simply referring to them in the notice of location thereof as being "about one-half mile from the Hurt mines, the direction being southwest."

Under the provisions of said Section 2324, Revised Statutes of the United States, and Section 3102, Revised Statutes of Idaho, reference may be made in a notice o° location of mining ground, to a located mining claim, as a mining claim is a natural object or landmark, or fixed object within the meaning of said provisions; but such reference must be reasonably certain, which was not so in the Magpie location notice. It has been frequently held that reference to well known mining claims is a sufficient compliance with the law. Hammer vs: Milling Co., 9 Sup. Ct., 548, 130 U. S., 291, 32 L. Ed., 964; Duncan vs. Fulton (Colo. App.), 61 Pac., 244; Kinney vs. Fleming (Ariz.), 56 Pac., 723. There are some early decisions to the contrary but the Supreme Courts of the United States, of Arizona and of Colorado, in the decisions above cited, hold as above stated.

It was inadvertently stated in the decision of Brown vs. Levan, supra, that the requirements of said Section 3102, Revised Statutes, in reference to naming the adjoining claims in the location notice, had been complied with, when the record shows that the mining claims named in said notice as adjoining claims, had not been located at that time. If they had been located prior to the location of the Magpie, reference to them as adjoining claims would have been a sufficient reference to a natural object, landmark, permanent monument, or fixed object to come within the provisions of said statutes, and the conclusion would have been different; for under the provisions of said Section 3102, Revised Statutes, reference might have been made to an adjoining claim as a natural landmark, fixed or permanent object as the natural object may adjoin or be upon the claim located for the law does not require that it be some distance from it. In the case o° Railroad Co. vs. San Garde, supra, this Court held that, as the location notice failed to give the direction of the mining claim from the mouth of "Big Canyon" (the natural object to which it was atte..pted to tie said mining claim), it failed to comply with the provision of the law in that regard, and adhered to the rule laid down in the case of Brown vs. Levan, supra. There the notice failed to give the direction of the claim from the fixed object to which an attempt was made to tie it.

We shall now recur to the location notice or certificate of said Bullion mining claim, and the ruling of the Court in refusing to admit it in evidence on the trial. The Court evidently rejected said notice upon an inspection of the notice itself. No evidence was permitted to be introduced as to the sufficiency or insufficiency of said notice, and no evidence by which the Court could determine whether the references and statements in said notice were true or not, or sufficient to render the situation or location of said mining claim reasonably certain from the letter of the notice itself, except the witness Shaw was permitted to testify that the Minnesota and Red Jacket mines mentioned in said notice were well known mines, and that the former was 100 by 600 feet. The location notice was rejected as being insufficient on its face. It is well established by numerous decisions that only where the insufficiency of the location certificate in its failure to make intelligent reference to natural objects or permanent landmarks, is apparent on its face, the Court may reject. Dillon vs. Bayliss, 11 Mont., 171, 27 Pac., 725; Darger vs. LeSieur (Utah), 30 Pac., 363; Hammer vs. Milling Co., 9 Sup. Ct., 548, 130 U. S., 291, 32 L. Ed., 964; Russel vs. Chumasero, 4 Mont., 309, 1 Pac., 713; Railroad Co. vs. San Garde (Idaho), 61 Pac., 137; Farmington Gold Min. Co. vs. Rhymney Gold and Copper Co. (Utah), 58 Pac., 832, 77 Am. St. Rep., 913; Flavin vs. Mattingly, 8 Mont., 242, 19 Pac., 384. Of course if there is a total failure to make any reference to such objects whatever, the certificate would not be sufficient.

The location certificate under consideration states that the Bullion claim is 600 feet in length along the vein or lode and 300 feet on each side thereof, commencing at a stake and notice situated about 300 feet in a northwesterly direction from the Minnesota mine; that it is an extension of the Red Jacket mine; and running thence along the vein or lode in a southerly direction to a similar stake and notice; and that the locators claim 600 linear feet in a southerly direction from this stake and notice to a similar stake and notice. It is stated in the notice that the Bullion is an extension of the Red Jacket mine, and runs thence along the vein or lode in a southerly direction. This description fixed the Bullion as a southerly extension of the Red Jacket, hence it adjoins that mine on the southerly end.

Said Section 2324, Revised Statutes of the United States, requires the certificate of location to contain the name of the locators, the date of the location and a description of the claim by reference to such natural object or permanent monument as will identify it; and said Section 3102, Revised Statutes, provides, among other things, that such certificate must contain such a description of the locality of the claim by reference to natural landmarks or fixed objects and contiguous claims, if there be any, as to render the situation reasonably certain from the letter of the notice itself. We think said notice on its face, contains a substantial compliance with said provisions, and the Court erred in not receiving it in evidence.

In Hammer vs. Milling Co., 9 Sup. Ct., 548, 130 U. S., 291, 32 L. Ed., 964, the certificate of location reads: "This lode is located about fifteen hundred feet south of Vaughn's Little Jennie mine." The Supreme Court of Montana held that that was a sufficient reference to a natural object or permanent monument, within the meaning of the provisions of the statutes. And the Supreme Court of the United States in sustaining that decision, said: "We agree with the Court below that the Little Jennie mine will be presumed to be a well known natural object or permanent monument until the contrary appears." In the case at bar it is made to appear by oral testimony that both the Minnesota and Red Jacket mines referred to in said notice of location are well known mines in that vicinity, and that the stake and notice first referred to therein are situated about 300 feet in a northwesterly direction from the Minnesota mine. So far as appears from the record, said Minnesota and Red Jacket mines may be patented mines, but that is not required as they are well known mines, in that vicinity. See Russell vs. Chumasero, 4 Mont., 309, 1 Pac., 713.

In Farmington Gold Min. Co. vs. Rhymney Gold and Copper Co. (Utah), 58 Pac., 832, 77 Am. St. Rep., 913, the certificate of location was quite loosely drawn and we think the correct rule in regard to the question under consideration was there laid down. In passing upon the sufficiency of that certificate, the Court said: "If by any reasonable construction, in view of the surrounding circumstances, the language employed in the description will impart notice to subsequent locators, it is sufficient."

As stated in that opinion, prospectors, as a rule make no pretensions of scholarship, are neither surveyors nor lawyers and if in their notices of location technical accuracy of expression was an absolute requirement the object of the law would in many cases be defeated and great injustice result by disturbing possession, after much hard labor has been performed, and money expended. We think the history of mining in this country shows that much more injustice has been done by depriving men who have in good faith, located valuable mines, and thereafter been deprived of them, by reason of some technical defect in their certificate of location than has resulted in the "floating" of claims, often referred to in the decisions of courts in this class of cases. A liberal construction should be given to location certificates and their sufficiency with reference to natural objects or permanent monuments is a question of fact, where natural objects or permanent monuments are referred to therein. Where the location certificate contains a reference to a landmark, it should not, upon a mere inspection of the certificate and in the absence of evidence, be declared insufficient, unless it clearly fails to identify the claims. Russell vs. Chumasero, supra; Hammer vs. Milling Co., supra; Flavin vs. Mattingly, 8 Mont., 242, 19 Pac., 384.

If the rule laid down in the case at bar in any manner conflicts with the rule laid down in case of Brown vs. Levan, supra, that case is overruled to the extent of such conflict; but the facts in that case show that the claims referred to as the "Hurt mines" were not situated with reference to the Magpie claim as stated in the location notice, and that the mining claims named as adjoining claims were not located until some time after the Magpie claim had been located and one of them never was located.

The second error relied upon is the refusal of the Court to receive the amended certificate of location in evidence. The Court refused to admit said certificate for the reason that the original certificate had been held void by the Court. As we have above held that the Court was in error in holding the original certificate void, it follows that the ground for refusing to admit the amended certificate was not well taken.

Section 5 of an act entitled, "An act to define the manner of locating lode, quartz and placer claims, * * * approved February 14, 1899. (Session Laws 1899, page 237) is as follows: 'If at any time the locator of any mining claim heretofore or hereafter located, or his assigns, shall apprehend that his original certificate was defective, erroneous or that the requirements of the law had not been complied with before filing or shall be desirous of changing the surface boundaries or of taking any part of an overlapping claim which has been abandoned, or in case the original certificate was made prior to the passage of this law, and he shall be desirous of securing the benefits of this act, such locator or his assigns, may file an additional certificate subject to the conditions of this act, and to contain all that this act required an original certificate to contain; Provided, That such amended location does not interfere with the existing rights of others at the time when such amendment is made.' That section provides for the amendment of original certificates of location, and provides that if the locator shall apprehend that his original certificate was defective, erroneous, or that the requirement of law had not been complied with, etc., such locator or his assigns may file an amended certificate curing such defects and such amended certificate relates back to the date of the original location, provided that it does not interfere with the existing rights of others. Most, if not all of the mining States have similar statutes, that have been considered and construed by the federal courts and the supreme courts of those States. From such statutes and the decisions under them, it is clear that an amended certificate may cure a defective or erroneous original certificate, and relates back to the date of the original certificate, except when such original certificate is absolutely void, or when the rights of others have intervened between the date of the original and amended locations.

First we shall consider whether a void original certificate can be amended. In McEvoy vs. Hyman (C.C.), 25 Fed., 596, the Circuit Court of the United States in discussing the right to amend, says: "Errors and mistakes in certificates of location are of frequent occurrence, under the law as it is at present, a fully complete and unimpeachable certificate cannot be made without the aid of a surveyor and the best instruments. It is often and perhaps generally, impracticable to obtain the services of a surveyor in making a location, and the miner must depend upon his own skill and judgment. In such effort he usually fails. Indeed, it may be said, as to the course of his lines, he is always in error, and the natural object and permanent monument required by Section 2324 are entirely beyond his grasp. He does not know what they are, nor how to refer to them. Every one who is at all familiar with mining locations knows that in practice the first record must usually, if not always, be imperfect. Recognizing these difficulties, it has never been the policy of the law to avoid a location for defects in the record, but rather to give the locator an opportunity to correct his record whenever defects may be found in it." And the Court there held that the section of the Colorado statutes which declares that defective certificates shall be void must be read in connection with the section authorizing amendments, and when so read the section will be construed as saying that defective certificates are lacking in force and sufficiency until amended, but are not wholly void. In Frisholm vs. Fitzgerald (Colo. Sup), 53 Pac., 1109, it was held that a mining claim location certificate, may be amended to cure failure to refer to a natural object or permanent monument, though between the filing of the original and amended certificate, another had filed on the claim. It would appear from this decision that no reference was made in the original certificate whatever to a permanent object. The section of the Colorado statute under consideration in that case was similar to our Section 5 above quoted, in that it provides for the correction of errors and defects occurring in the original certificate, and it authorizes a change of boundaries or taking in of territory not included in the original certificate and the Court in that case says: "The plain purport and effect of the first clause is to enable the miner who in good faith has gone upon the public domain and expended time and money in performing the substantial acts required to locate a mining claim, but through inadvertance or ignorance has failed to comply with the requirements of the statute in describing his claim, to cure such error at any time by an amendment correcting the defective description, and thus perfect his record as of the date of the original certificate. We do not understand that the proviso has reference to amendments of this character but is only applicable to a change of boundaries and relocation that shall take in territory not before included within the claim," although Campbell vs. C. J. and Gabbert J., state in a concurring opinion, that they express no opinion in regard to the construction of said statute. The rule there laid down is clearly the one applicable to the provisions of said Section 5, and with that construction those provisions may be made to protect the rights of the locator, without prejudicing any interests that third parties have rightfully acquired. In Strepey vs. Stark, 7 Colo., 614, 5 Pac., 111, it is said: "And even when the certificate for any of the resons set forth in the statute is deemed void, it has been admissible in evidence with a valid amended certificate correcting the defects of the original." See also, Van Zandt vs. Mining Co. (C. C.), 8 Fed., 725, 2 McCrary, 159; Jordon vs. Sherman (Ariz.), 53 Pac., 579; Moyle vs. Bullene (Colo. App.), 44 Pac., 69.

The above cited decisions are from Colorado, a state where there is a statutory provision which declares that, where the certificate fails to describe the claim, with reference to some natural object or permanent monument it is void. We have no such provision. This Court is in accord with the rule laid down in those decisions upon the question under consideration here. If in making the amended location it included land not included in the original location and interfered with existing rights as to such land, the amended location would not relate back to the date of the original location, so far as the recently included land is concerned. The record shows that the amended location was made by one having authority to make such location. Such authority is not required to be in writing.

We have examined assignments of error numbered from 3 to 10, inclusive, and concluded that the Court erred in not admitting the evidence referred to in said assignments. The trial Court, however, took the view that the original certificate of location was absolutely void and on that ground rejected said evidence.

It follows that the Court erred in granting the non-suit, and the judgment is reversed, and the cause remanded for further proceedings. Costs of the appeal are awarded to the appellants.

Quarles. C. J., and Stockslager. J., concur.

# CHAPTER III.

Correct answers to a few practical and pertinent questions are, after all, of greater value to the every day prospector and miner than any cold statement of the law can possibly be. In this chapter an attempt has been made to cover the subject by answers to questions dealing with the details most likely to confront or vex the seeker after mineral wealth in the appropriation of claims believed to contain them. The index, at the end of this volume, will be a guide for the user of this work in directing him to a solution of the question requiring it.

## QUESTIONS AND ANSWERS.

Question 1.    How shall I proceed to locate a quartz claim in Idaho?
Answer.    Upon making a discovery of a quartz lode or vein, erect a monument at the point of discovery, write thereon the name of the claim, the date of discovery and distance claimed along the vein each way, from such discovery monument, and your name. Within ten days from making such discovery and posting such notice, mark the boundaries of your claim by establishing at each corner thereof and at any angle in the side lines, a monument marked with the name of the claim and the corner or angle it represents; at the time of so marking the boundaries, you should post at your discovery monument, your notice of location, which should contain the name of the claim, the direction and distance claimed each way along the vein from the discovery, the distance claimed on each side of the middle of the vein, the distance and direction from the discovery monument to such natural object or permanent monument as will fix and describe in the notice itself the location of the claim, the name of the mining district, the county, State, name of claim and name of locator, date of discovery and date of location. Your monuments should be at least four feet high above the ground and when made of trees or posts they should be hewn and marked upon the side facing towards the discovery and must be at least four inches square or in diameter. A good manner of posting the notice is to write your notice of location upon a piece of smoothed board with lead pencil and nail it to the discovery stake, or secure and conspicuously fasten it to the discovery monument if made of stone; or you can smooth the discovery stake upon one side and write the notice legibly upon it with lead pencil. A notice so written will last many years. Within sixty days of posting your location notice, you must sink a shaft on the lode or ledge, not less than ten feet in depth measured from the lowest part of the rim of the shaft at the surface, to the bottom of the shaft, and of not less than sixteen square feet area, that is four by four in surface area, and of one hundred and sixty cubic feet. See that your shaft is the same area all the way down, and as deep in the corners at the bottom as it is in the middle. A copy of the location notice, as near as possible like the one posted on your discovery stake must be filed with the County Recorder or the deputy recorder appointed or acting in the district in which the claim is situated and pay the proper fee for recording. This copy of your location notice must be filled within ninety days of location-discovery. If you have made a valid discovery of mineral and followed these steps in locating it, your location is complete. For further guidance study the following diagram of a claim and location notice fully complying with the law.

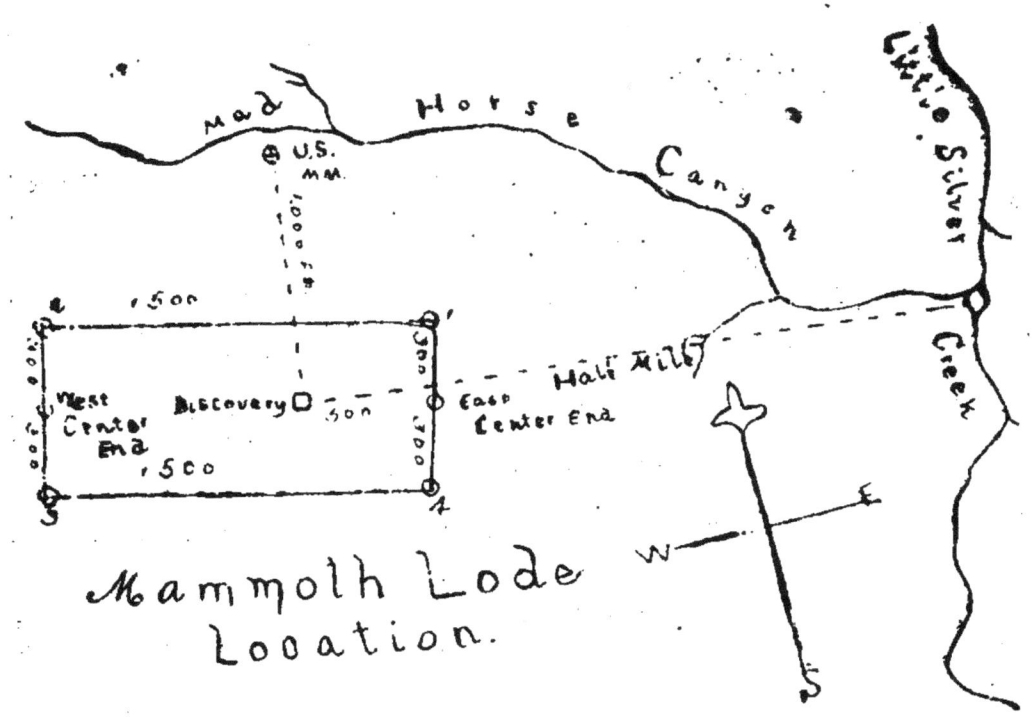

Mammoth Lode Location.

## NOTICE OF LOCATION.

Notice is hereby given that I, the undersigned, a citizen of the United States of America, having complied with the requirements of Chapter Six of Title Thirty-two of the Revised Statutes of the United States, and of the laws of the State of Idaho, relating to the location of mining claims, and all local customs, laws and regulations, have located fifteen hundred linear feet along this lode or vein of quartz, bearing gold, silver, lead, copper and other precious metals, by three hundred feet in width on each side of the lode, making six hundred feet in width.

This claim is called and named the Mammoth and is situated on the south side of Mad Horse Canyon, half a mile west from its entrance into Little Silver Creek Canyon, in Neal Mining District, County of Elmore, and State of Idaho, and is described as follows:

Commencing at the discovery stake and notice, which is situated one thousand feet south from United States Mineral Monument No. 1, thence from said stake and notice running east 500 feet to east center end stake; thence north 300 feet to Corner No. 1; thence west 1500 feet to Corner No. 2; thence south 300 feet to west center end stake; thence south 300 feet to Corner No. 3; thence east 1500 feet to Corner No. 4; thence north 300 feet to east center end stake, being the place of beginning of exterior boundaries of said claim.

The distance claimed along this lode or vein each way from the discovery stake and notice is five hundred feet east and one thousand feet west from said stake and notice.

Discovered this 1st day of April, 1899.

Located this 1st day of April, 1899.

JOHN SMITH, Locator.

At or about the time when you record above notice of location, you must subscribe and swear to the following affidavit, which should be on or attached to the notice:

State of Idaho,    )
                   )  ss.
County of Elmore.  )

I, John Smith, do solemnly swear that I am a citizen of the United States (or have declared my intentions to become such) and that I am acquainted with the mining ground described in this notice of location and herewith called the Mammoth ledge, lode or claim; that the claim and ground therein described or any part thereof has not, to the best of my knowledge and belief, been located according to the laws of the United States and of this State, or if so located, that the same has been abandoned and forfeited by reason of a failure of such former locators to comply in respect thereto with the requirements of said laws, and that I have opened new ground to the extent and depth of ten feet as required by the laws of Idaho.

JOHN SMITH.

Subscribed and sworn to before me this 2nd day of May, A. D. 1899.
(Seal.)                        WILLIAM JONES,
                        Notary Public, County of Elmore.

The following will do as a form for your first or ten days' notice of location, that is to say, that one which is posted after discovery and before corner stakes are erected:

To whom it may concern: Notice—I, the undersigned, John Smith, do hereby claim 500 feet easterly and 1000 feet westerly from this discovery stake and notice along this vein or lode, bearing gold, silver, lead, copper and other precious metals and 300 feet on each side of the center thereof. Name of claim, the Mammoth, discovered this 1st day of April, 1899.

JOHN SMITH, Locator.

Question 2.    Must I post the preliminary or ten days' notice before posting my permanent notice of location?

Answer.    If at the time of discovery you are able to determine your boundaries and properly tie your claim, you may omit the preliminary notice and post only the permanent notice, otherwise it is advisable to post the preliminary notice. In most cases it requires some work and further prospecting to determine the true course of a lead, and by posting the preliminary notice you have ten days further in which to more fully ascertain these facts and perfect the boundaries of the claim.

Question 3.    Must I sink a ten-foot shaft in order to make a valid location? Or can I make the location in this respect by driving an adit or tunnel in upon the vein.

Answer.    The Statute uses the following language: "Any excavation which shall cut such vein ten feet from the lowest part of the rim of such shaft and which shall measure 160 cu. ft. in extent shall be considered a compliance with this provision." The Statute is somewhat ambiguous in this respect, as is evident by the foregoing, but it is the opinion of the Author that an open cut extended into the mountain a distance of ten feet and attaining a ten-foot depth at the face of the cut and exposing the vein or ledge and making an excavation of not less than 160 cu. ft. would be considered by the Courts, the equivalent of the ten-foot shaft, but I would advise the performance in each case of a little more work than seems to be required rather than less, as valuable mining property has sometimes been lost by reason of failure to make the full amount of excavation as required by Statute.

**Question 4.** In the event that I am unable to tie my claim to a mineral monument or Government corner, how shall I proceed to comply with the laws in this respect?

**Answer.** If you can afford the expense, get a surveyor to establish a mineral monument in the neighborhood of your claim; otherwise, use any of the following methods: Measure the distance from your discovery stake to the point where two well known creeks come together and having established the course and distance to this point, use it for the purpose. Or use the mouth of some well known gulch or stream within convenient distance, or the top of some nearby mountain peak, or a corner of a patented claim, if there is one in your neighborhood, or a large and distinct tree, hewing well the side towards your claim and carving in the hewn part, the letters B. T. Mammoth Lode, or you may use a prominent butte or ledge or projecting rock, carving thereon the letters B. M. Mammoth Lode. You cannot use too much care as to this duty in completing your location as both the Federal and State law require the description as to the locality of the claim to be certain and easily to be identified from the description in the location notice itself, and the Supreme Court of Idaho, in the case of Levan versus Brown, made a very rigid construction of the Statute in this respect, and a want of certainty or sufficiency in this matter may result in your losing a valuable claim.

**Question 5.** How shall I mark the corner and center stakes of the claim?

**Answer.** By marking on them distinctly on the side towards the claim the number and character of the stake and the name of the claim, for instance: Corner No. 1. Mammoth Lode or West Center End Stake, Mammoth Lode.

**Question 6.** A., B. and C. each owns a quartz claim, the three claims being contiguous; B. and C. each deeds his claim to A., so that A. now owns the three claims. Can A. divide the one hundred dollars' worth of work, placing one-third on each of the claims and claim a compliance with the laws as to annual assessment work?

**Answer.** No. A. may treat them as one claim, but the law will not so consider them, but will require the full one hundred dollars' worth of work on each claim annually, or three hundred dollars' worth of work expended on one claim, pursuant to a system of development for the benefit of all the claims.

**Question 7** .Having completed my location, when shall I be required to again do work upon my claim?

**Answer.** You will have all of the year following that in which you made your location in which to do your first annual assessment work of the value of $100 or the same value of improvements upon your claim.

**Question 8.** How shall I locate a placer claim?

**Answer.** Place a substantial post, stake, or monument, as required in locating quartz claims, at each corner of your location. In the notice of location, which you post conspicuously on one of these stakes or monuments, you tie the stake or monument on which it is placed to some natural object or permanent monument as in the case of lode claims. Within fifteen days after making the location you must make an excavation on your claim, removing therefrom not less then one hundred cubic feet of ground for the purpose of prospecting. Within thirty days after making your location, you must file for record with the County Recorder or the deputy mining Recorder of the district, a copy of the notice of location, subscribing before some person authorized to administer oaths, an affidavit, similar in form as in the case of quartz claims, which affidavit is on or attached to the notice of location. The following form is recommended and may be used with safety in placer locations:

## PLACER LOCATION NOTICE.

Notice is hereby given that I, the undersigned, John Doe, a citizen of the United States of America, having complied with the requirements of Chapter Six of Title Thirty-two of the Revised Statutes of the United States, and the laws of the State of Idaho, relating to the location of mining claims and all local customs, laws and regulations, have located twenty acres of placer mining ground. The claim or location is hereby named the "Silent Hope," is 600 feet wide by 1500 feet in length, and is situated on the west slope of Bald Nigger Butte, and one and a half miles west of the mouth of Wild Horse Canyon, in the Never Despair Mining District, County of Elmore and State of Idaho, and is more particularly described as follows, to-wit: Commencing at this discovery stake and notice, marked Corner No. 1, which is situated 900 feet west of a lone pine tree about 14 inches in diameter and hewn on the side facing this claim and marked B. T. on the crest of Bald Nigger Butte, and quarter of a mile north of the mouth of Pickaninny Creek, running thence from this corner north 600 feet to Corner No. 2, a stake, thence west 1500 feet to Corner No 3, a stone monument, thence south 600 feet to Corner No. 4, stake, thence east 1500 feet to Corner No. 1, the place of beginning of the exterior boundaries of this claim, each and all of said boundary stakes and monument being duly marked and erected as required by law. The mining locations contiguous to this claim are the "W. J. B.," a placer claim, on the west, the "Bimetallic," a lode claim on the northwest, the "Constitution" on the south and the "Imperialist" on the northeast.

Discovered this 1st day of May, 1899.

Located this 1st day of May, 1899.

JOHN DOE, Locator.

The affidavit which must be subscribed as above directed, and which is attached to the notice of location, may be as follows:

State of Idaho,  
County of Elmore.  } ss.

I, John Doe, do solemnly swear that I am a citizen of the United States (or have declared my intentions to become such) and that I am acquainted with the mining ground described in this notice of location and herewith called the "Silent Hope," deposit or placer claim; that the claim and ground therein described or any part thereof, has not to the best of my knowledge and belief, been located according to the laws of the United States and of this State, or if so located, that the same has been abandoned and forfeited by reason of the failure of such former locator to comply in respect thereto, with the requirements of said laws and that I have opened new ground by means of excavation to the extent of one hunderd cubic feet as required by the laws of Idaho.

JOHN DOE.

Subscribed and sworn to before me this 13th day of May, A. D. 1899.
(Seal.)                     WILLIAM K. JONES.
                        Notary Public, County of Elmore.

Remember, also that if your claim is situated upon lands that have been surveyed by the United States, the lines of your claim should conform to the legal subdivisions, and you should so designate the claim in your notice, as for instance: "The south half of the northwest quarter of the northeast quarter of Section 3, Township 5, North of Range 8 West, Boise Meridian," in addition to staking, tying etc., as on unsurveyed land.

Question 9.     An association of eight persons located 160 acres placer claim. Must $100 worth of work or improvements be annually expended as assessment work upon each twenty acres thereof?

Answer.     No. The law permits an association of eight persons to take up as one claim, 160 acres of placer ground, and the construction of the Courts has been that as to annual assessment work it may be treated as one claim.

Question 10.     Of what should the labor and improvements necessary to be made or expended annually, consist?

Answer.     That is quite well answered by Land Commissioner Williamson, in a communication to the Surveyor-General of Colorado, as follows: "All improvements made upon a mining claim having a direct relation to the development thereof may be taken in consideration: Any building, machinery, wagon road or other improvement used in connection with, and essential to the practical development of the claim. Necessarily, however, improvements of the character indicated must be associated with actual excavation such as cuts, tunnels, shafts, etc., so as to clearly show that they are intended for use in connection with the claim under consideration."

Question 11.     I have three placer claims, A., B. and C. I construct a reservoir on claim A. from which to conduct water solely for use on claim C. Can the value of the work and improvement of the reservoir constitute and be considered assessment work on claim A.?

Answer.     No. The work and value of the improvement on A. is not intended for the benefit of the claim, or as an improvement thereon and cannot therefore apply.

Question 12.     During the year, at different times, I have been picking small quantities of rock and ore from the ledge in my claim for sampling purposes, crushing, panning and assaying. Can this work be credited on my annual assessment work?

Answer.     No. This neither adds to the development or value of the claim.

Question 13.     Can money and time expended in arranging for putting improvements upon the claim be credited on assessment work?

Answer.     No.

Question 14.     Can the cost of construction of buildings constructed on my quartz claim and for its use and improvement, be credited on annual assessment work?

Answer.     It has been so held where such construction is intimately connected with the operation and development of the claim. It is, however, unsafe to rely wholly on such improvements as being sufficient in themselves to constitute the work or improvements contemplated by the statute.

Question 15.    Can I include more than one quartz claim in one location notice?

Answer.         No. Such a location would be wholly void.

Question 16.    Should I find after locating a quartz claim that its boundaries are not as they should be, that the claim is not tied to a natural object or permanent monument with sufficient certainty, or should I desire to embrace in my claim a portion of other ground and abandon part of my present claim, or should there exist any other defect in the location thereof which I wish to remedy, but which does not make the location of the claim wholly void, how shall I proceed?

Answer.         By making an amended location, and re-establishing your claim boundaries. And by duly posting the original amended and filing for record your copy of amended certificate of location, but by such amended location you cannot acquire any right to any portion of any claim then held by valid location made prior to your amended location.

The following is a good form for the additional certificate of an amended location, which may be used in substance for either lode or placer amended locations.

## AMENDED LOCATION CERTIFICATE.

Know all men by these presents: That I, John Smith, the undersigned, a citizen of the United States of America, over the age of twenty-one years, having complied with the laws of the United States and of the State of Idaho, relating to mining claims, and with the local laws, customs and regulations of the Neal Mining District, hereby make and file for record this amended location of the Mammoth (in case of change of name say, at one time and formerly the Gray Horse) Lode, claiming by right of discovery, location, appropriation and possession fifteen hundred feet, linear and horizontal measurement, on this vein, ledge, or lode of quartz, or other rock in place bearing gold, silver, lead, copper and other precious minerals along the course of said vein or lode with all dips, variations, spurs and angles thereof, the same being 500 feet in an easterly direction from the discovery stake and notice and 1000 feet in a westerly direction therefrom and 300 feet in width on each side of the middle of said vein or lode at the surface, making a total of 600 feet in width, and all veins, lodes, ledges, mineral deposits, mineral and surface ground within the lines of said claim.

This claim is situate in Neal Mining District, County of Elmore, and State of Idaho, on the south side of Mad Horse Canyon, half a mile west from its entrance into Little Silver Creek Canyon, and is more particularly described as follows, to-wit: Commencing at the discovery stake and notice, which is situated one thousand feet south from United States Mineral Monument No. 1 from said stake and notice, running thence east 500 feet to east center end stake, thence north 300 feet to Corner No. 1, thence west 1500 feet to Corner No. 2, thence south 300 feet to west center end stake, thence south 300 feet to Corner No. 3, thence east 1500 feet to Corner No. 4, thence north 300 feet to east center end stake, being the place of beginning of exterior boundaries of said claim.

The claims lying and being contiguous to this claim and location are the Sweet Alice on the north, the Termagant on the south, the Mastodon on the east, and the Marsupial on the west.

This amended location is made in conformity with the original location made the 1st day of April, 1899, recorded the 15th day of April, 1899, in Book........ of Quartz Locations, at page........ in the office of the Recorder of said County, and it is made for the purpose of appropriating all ground within the boundaries hereinbefore described, and of more definitely describing the situation and boundaries of said lode, correcting any irregularities or errors and supplying any defects which may have existed in the original location, or the record thereof, and to secure all the benefits of Section 5 of the act of the Legislature found on Page 24 of the laws of the Third Session of the Idaho Legislature, hereby waiving no rights acquired under and by virtue of said original location, discovery and possession of said claim.

Date of original location April 1, 1899.

Date of amended location April 20, 1899.

JOHN SMITH, Locator.

### AFFIDAVIT..

State of Idaho, } ss.
County of Elmore, }

I, John Smith, do solemnly swear that I am a citizen of the United States of America (or have declared my intention to become such) and that I am acquainted with the mining ground described in this amended notice of location and herewith called the Mammoth lode, ledge or claim; that the ground and claim therein described or any part thereof has not to the best of my knowledge and belief been located according to the laws of the United States and of this State, save as mentioned in the within notice, or if so located that the same has been abandoned or forfeited by reason of the failure of such former locators to comply in respect thereto with the requirements of said laws, that I am the original locator of said claim or (that I am the owner and entitled to the possession of an assigned interest in said claim.)

JOHN SMITH.

Subscribed and sworn to before me this 20th day of April, A. D. 1899.

WILLIAM JONES,
Notary Public, County of Elmore.

Question 17.     In making an amended location, suppose A. has prior thereto, but subsequent to the making of my original location, located an adjoining claim, conflicting in part with my original claim. In making my amended location, I still retain within my lines the part in conflict. Would this portion then become part of A.'s claim or mine?

Answer.     It would be a part of your claim as covered and defined territorially by your amended location notice and stakes set as mentioned therein. A. never had any title or possession of the part in conflict; in order to get it, even in event that you abandoned your claim, he would have to make a new location to cover that part in conflict.

Question 18.     I own two or more lode claims and wish to perform the annual assessment work for them all on one of the claims Can I do so and fully comply with the law?

Answer.     Yes, provided that you own each of the claims you wish so to represent, and that the claims are contiguous, and provided, further, that the work prosecuted and performed on the one claim actually benefits each of them, and is pursuant to a general plan of development for all the claims and in value in the aggregate sufficient to represent $100 for each claim.

Question 19.     But suppose I own one claim and A. owns the adjoining claim. Can we unite and jointly do $200 worth of labor on the one claim, pursuant to a general plan of development for the benefit of both, and have that work credited as assessment work on each claim?

Answer.          No. There must be a community of interests or privity of ownership in each and all the claims to be so benefited, as well as in the work and plan of development.

Question 20.     But suppose that while the record title of one claim is in me, and of a second claim in A., and of a third claim in B. and that we have an oral agreement by which we have a joint ownership in each of the claims, and own and work them for our mutual benefit. In that event would sufficient work done jointly by myself, A. and B. and pursuant to a general plan of development for all the claims be deemed a sufficient compliance with the law?

Answer.          Yes. But you would have to show that the community of interests or, in other words, that the agreement referred to, was made and existed prior to the time of performing such labor, and that the work done was in sufficient amount and beneficial to each of the claims thereby represented.

Question 21.     I have a number of claims adjoining each other in one group, and wish to develop them all by running a tunnel and drifting therefrom in each claim, as a tunnel approaches it. The entrance and some part of the tunnel is, however, situated at a point outside of any of my group of claims. Can the work done in the tunnel be credited on assessment to represent each of the group so owned and developed?

Answer.          Yes. Provided that it is in value sufficient to represent each claim separately, otherwise only to value of work so done.

Question 22.     Can I run a tunnel starting on a patented claim owned by me, the tunnel being run in accordance with a system of development beneficial to each of a group of unpatented, claims also owned by me? Would the work in said tunnel, if sufficient in value be credited as full assessment work on each of the unpatented group?

Answer.          Yes.

Question 23.     I own a placer claim and construct a ditch for the purpose of carrying water on to and thereby working it. So far as present constructed the ditch is not on the claim. Can I credit the value of work done on said ditch in this year against my annual assessment work for this year?

Answer.          Yes. Such is the weight of authority.

Question 24.     Would the cost for the survey of such ditch, no part thereof ever having been constructed, apply to the amount of the value and cost of such survey to annual assessment work on the placer claim?

Answer.          No.

Question 25.     Will the cost of constructing a dam or reservoir, made for the purpose of storing and conducting water on to my placer claim, apply as annual assessment thereon?

**Answer.**        Yes.

**Question 25.**    I own three placer claims. On the lower one I construct a flume for the purpose of carrying away tailings from the claims more elevated. On which of these claims, if any, can I lawfully credit the cost of constructing such flume as annual assessment work?

**Answer.**        On the claim for the benefit of which it was constructed. If it benefits two claims and was constructed for the purpose of so doing, then the cost of its construction must be in amount sufficient to represent each of them before you can credit it on those two claims as full assessment, or there must be other work on the claim on which the amount is sufficient in value to make up such deficiency.

**Question 26.**    I construct a wagon road for the benefit of my claim, in part on it, and in connection with the active work thereon, can I credit the cost of this road to annual assessment work?

**Answer.**        Yes. The decisions are to that effect. However, the safer way is not to rely on such work alone.

**Question 27.**    I locate a claim and in addition to the work necessary to perfect my location, and during that year I perform $100 worth of work. Can I credit the value of such labor to the first annual labor necessary to be performed?

**Answer.**        No. The annual labor required to be done or improvements necessary to be made upon a claim each year after location and before application for patent, must be done or made in the necessary amount during the year which it is intended to represent. The work done to perfect your location will hold your claim until the 31st day of December in the succeeding year.

**Question 28.**    During the year A. goes upon my claim and without my knowledge or consent performs $100 worth of work. Can I apply that work on my annual assessment of labor?

**Answer.**        No.

**Question 29.**    If I afterwards pay A. for his labor, can I then credit it on annual assessment?

**Answer.**        No. The work must be done at the instance of yourself or some one in privity with you.

**Question 30.**    I purchase a lode claim from A. who has in the current year performed his annual assessment work. Do I have to perform another $100 worth of work or same value of improvements in order to hold the claim?

**Answer.**        No.

**Question 31.**    Will the work in the year of such purchase and in prior years after location by A. count in the work required to procure United States patent?

**Answer.**        Yes. You succeed to the extent of your purchase to all A.'s right, development and title in the claim.

**Question 32.**    A. has attempted to relocate my claim, which I have never forfeited or abandoned, and now holds possession of it by force and by threats of violence prevents me going upon it and doing the labor necessary for the year. Must I at any hazard do this work?

**Answer.**        No. If you are satisfied A. is not bluffing, the law will excuse its performance. However, you should at once consult some reputable attorney as to the steps to be taken by you to regain possession. Every day's unnecessary delay will count against you with the court and jury whenever you do begin proceedings.

Question 33.    I have the annual work done upon my claim, but fail to pay the one who performed it. Will my failure to pay for such work defeat my claim to have it credited as annual assessment work?

Answer.         No. You have had the work done. Whether you do or are able to pay for it is not in question.

Question 34.    Is there any test as to what constitutes $100 worth of work?

Answer.         No. That is to say, the value of the work can neither be determined by its consisting of any fixed number of feet of shaft or tunnel work, nor can it be determined by what you pay for it. The law requires $100 worth of work or the same value of improvements, and the work to count for the purpose required must be worth in the district in which your claim is situated not less than $100.

Question 35.    I perform the annual assessment work and labor required on my claim, but failed to file the statutory affidavit thereof within the time designated by law. A. has jumped or relocated my claim, claiming forfeiture. Will my failure to file the affidavit defeat my claim to the property?

Answer.         No. Consult a good attorney as to getting possession again. Should a contest ensue, you will have to establish that you did in fact perform, or have others for you perform, the work in value as required, the burden of proof being upon you in such case.

Question 36.    I have applied for a patent on my claim, have made final entry and final receiver's receipt has issued. Pending the delay in the land office, on account of press of business, must I still perform annual labor?

Answer.         No.

Question 37.    Are mill sites subject to annual labor law?

Answer.         No.

Question 38.    A. discovers and locates a ledge of quartz, but fails to perform his annual assessment work. I relocate the claim; must I make a new discovery of the ledge in order to perfect my location?

Answer.         No. You may make your discovery at the same point of the vein uncovered by A. Remember, however, you must open up new ground to the extent or depth of ten feet as in a new location, which may be done in A.'s abandoned workings.

Question 39.    I have failed to perform annual labor upon my claim, but on the 1st day of January in each year, I have made a new location thereof. Can I so hold the claim indefinitely?

Answer.         If you can for one year, you can for any number of years. You cannot, however, in this way maintain your right to the claim as against subsequent locators, unless you follow up each relocation with a diligent performance of labor or improvements sufficient in value to meet the requirements of annual labor for the ensuing year. By doing so you would hold the property not by virtue of relocation, but on the strength of having resumed work thereon as permitted and recognized by United States law, the work applying on your first, not your second location. Were it otherwise, the intent and spirit of the law which requires annual assessment and development would be defeated. Although the Supreme Court of Utah has held to the contrary, it is not expected that that decision will obtain or be binding on other courts, or be accepted as the law on the question.

**Question 40.** I quit-claim my mining claim to A. who subsequently forfeits by failure to do annual labor. May I then relocate the claim?

**Answer.** Yes. A. having obtained all your title and interest in the claim, you have as good a right as any other stranger to relocate it upon A.'s forfeiture or abandonment.

**Question 41.** A. employs me to do the annual labor on his claim. Having failed to do so and with the intent by such neglect to defraud him of his claim, I on the 1st day of January, relocate the claim for myself. Can I hold it?

**Answer.** No. Any interest or title obtained by you in that way to the property will be deemed to be held in trust for A. and for his benefit.

**Question 42.** I own a quartz claim jointly with A. We employ B. to do the annual labor. B. instigated by and in collusion with A. fails to carry out his agreement. On the first day of the following January B. relocates the claim in his own name pursuant to an agreement with A..., by which B. agrees to deed A. a half interest therein. Have I any title or interest in the property after such relocation?

**Answer.** You have exactly the same interest in the property as you had previously to the relocation. B. has no interest therein, and holds the title to the property in trust for you and A.

**Question 43.** I have given a mortgage on my claim. Can I defeat the lien of the mortgage by intentionally forfeiting or abandoning the property, under an agreement with a friend whereby he relocates it in his own name and subsequently deeds me an interest?

**Answer.** No.

**Question 44.** How shall I relocate an abandoned or forfeited claim?

**Answer.** In the same manner you would in the case of an original location, except that you need not make a new discovery and need not sink a new discovery shaft, but may, if you see fit, sink the old discovery shaft ten feet further and of the same area in cubic feet as would be required in an original location.

**Question 45.** A. forfeits and I relocate his mining claim. Can I hold all A.'s improvements in the nature of fixtures on the premises?

**Answer.** Yes. All that A. has not removed prior to your relocation.

**Question 46.** A. procures a patent to his placer claim, but does not include in his application therefor a well known vein or lode that exists within the territorial boundaries of his placer. Can I thereafter locate that lode or vein?

**Answer.** Yes.

Question 47.     In such case how much surface ground would I be entitled to the use of?

Answer.          You would be entitled only to so much of the surface as is necessary in the working and operation of the lode.

Question 48.     I am a citizen, but under the age of twenty-one. Can I locate a mining claim?

Answer.          Yes. Age is not a pre-requisite for a valid location. There might arise a question, however, as to the interests in the property if you are dependent upon your parents for support and maintenance and under their control. You would also find some difficulties in making a conveyance of the claim or any part of it, should you desire to do so.

Question 49.     Not being a citizen and not having declared my intentions of becoming one, can I locate a mining claim?

Answer.          No.

Question 50.     Not being a citizen and not having declared intentions of becoming one, I jointly with A. locate a mining claim, which we afterwards jointly deed to N. Is N.'s title to the property good?

Answer.          Yes.

Question 51.     I am a woman. Can I make a valid location of a mining claim?

Answer.          Yes. In this matter the law gives no preference to sexes.

Question 52.     I have expended over $100 in annual labor on a claim owned jointly by myself and A. He now refuses to pay me for his share in such work. How must I proceed?

Answer.          You should advertise him out. Consult some good attorney in the matter for details of procedure.

Question 53.     Must I make a new discovery in making a relocation?

Answer.          No.

Question 54.     I have expended $100 in annual labor and improvements on a claim owned jointly by myself and A. He refuses to pay his proportion thereof. Can I advertise him out at once?

Answer.          Not until the expiration of the year within and for which such annual labor was done and improvements made. A. has to, and inclusive of, the 31st day of December of that year within which to do his share of the work.

Question 55.     Can an Idaho corporation locate a mining claim?

Answer.          Yes.

Question 56.     How shall I proceed to locate a mill site?

Answer.          The laws of Idaho do not make any provisions or regulations for the location of mill sites. The authority for such location is found in Section 2337, Revised Statutes of United States, the full text of which section is found in this work. Noticing that it is provided in that section that mill sites shall be subject to the same preliminary requirements as to notice, survey, etc., as are veins, or lodes, you should follow as nearly as practicable, the laws and customs governing the location of quartz claims; that is, in posting notice and afterwards recording it and the affidavit attached, staking the site and making improvements thereon as an evidence of good faith. Use following form of notice and affidavit:

### NOTICE OF LOCATION OF MILL SITE.

Take Notice: I, the undersigned, Sarsfield Dooley, a citizen of the

United States of America (or have declared my intentions to become such) over the age of 21 years, having complied with the laws of the United States relating to the location of mill sites, and all local customs, laws and regulations, have located this ground and claim as the Pachyderm Mill Site, the ground and claim hereby named and located as a mill site, to the best of my knowledge, information and belief, or any part thereof, having no lode, ledge or lead, bearing any valuable metals thereon and having no deposits therein of any such minerals, and being in extent not to exceed five acres, to be used as mill site in connection with my quartz ledge or lode named the "Mammoth" (or if independent of a quartz claim, to secure the said ground and claim for the erection of a quartz mill or reduction works), said ground and mill site being located in the "Seven Devils" mining district, County of Washington and State of Idaho, and bounded and described as follows, to-wit:

Beginning at this stake and notice, which is marked Corner No. 1 and which is situated 500 feet south of United States mineral monument No. 2 in said district and county, and 800 feet east of the southeast corner of my said Mammoth Quartz Claim, and running thence north 300 feet to Corner No. 2, thence west 750 feet to Corner No. 3, thence south 300 feet to Corner No. 4, thence east 750 feet to Corner No. 1, the place of beginning of the exterior boundaries of said mill site location; each and all said corners being staked according to law. Said mill site lying 50 feet east of the eastern boundary line of my said "Mammoth" claim.

Located this 10th day of May, 1899.

SARSFIELD DOOLEY. Locator.

## AFFIDAVIT.

State of Idaho,
County of Washington, } ss.

I, Sarsfield Dooley, do solemnly swear that I am a citizen of the United States of America (or have declared my intention to become such), that I am acquainted with the ground and claim described in the preceding notice of location as a mill site, called the "Pachyderm" mill site, and that to the best of my knowledge, information and belief has no valuable deposits of mineral thereon; that the said ground and claim is to be used and occupied by me, the proprietor of the "Mammoth" lode or ledge, for mining and milling purposes in connection with my said "Mammoth" lode (or that the said ground and claim so located as a mill site is to be used by me for the purpose of erecting and operating a quartz mill or reduction works thereon); that the said ground and claim has not, to the best of my knowledge and belief, been located according to the laws of the United States and of this State, or if so located, that the same has been abandoned and forfeited by reason of the failure of such former locators to comply in respect thereto with the requirements of such laws, and that I have located said mill site for the purposes in this notice and affidavit mentioned, and no other.

SARSFIELD DOOLEY,

Subscribed and sworn to before me this 12th day of May, A. D. 1899.
(Seal.)                            WILLIAM JONES.

Notary Public, County of Washington.

Question 57. My mill site abuts against end lines of my quartz location. Does that fact affect the validity of its location?

Answer.          It may affect it.  The presumption is that it contains or
                 covers the extension of the lode or ledge, which presump-
tion you will have to rebut when you apply for a patent, or in case of
a contest.

Question 58.     How would it be where the mill site abuts on the side
                 line of my quartz location?

Answer.          There would be no presumption in such case that it
                 covered a continuation of the lode.

Question 59.     I own a lode claim and mill site contiguous thereto,
                 and have done $500 worth of labor on my lode claim and
no work on the mill site, but use it for milling purposes.  Is the work
done sufficient to entitle me to patent on both claims?

Answer.          Yes.

Question 60.     Must I do location or assessment work on my mill site
                 to hold it?

Answer.          Not as such.  You should, however, occupy the claim
                 and place improvements for mining and milling purposes
                 thereon sufficient to show good faith .

Question 61.     How shall I proceed to locate a tunnel site?

Answer.          By placing at the mouth of the tunnel, at or before it
                 enters cover, a substantial stake or monument and plac-
ing thereon your location notice, by placing stakes or monuments along
the proposed line of your tunnel at a distance apart of not to exceed
500 feet, so as to clearly define such center, and tying the stake fur-
thest from the mouth of your tunnel on the proposed line thereof to
some natural object or permanent monument in the same manner as
in tying a quartz location by placing stakes or monuments at each
corner or angle of the exterior boundary of the ground enclosed and
claimed by your location marking such stakes and having them of a
size and height above ground as required in other locations and by
duly recording a copy of the notice and affidavit attached thereto.  The
following form of location notice and affidavit is recommended:

## TUNNEL SITE LOCATION NOTICE.

Notice is hereby given, that I, the undersigned, Frank Smith, a
citizen of the United States of America (or having declared my intention to become a citizen of the United States of America) having
complied with the laws of the United States and of the State of Idaho,
and all local rules, and customs, do hereby locate a tunnel site, to be
known as the "X Ray" tunnel site, for the better development of lodes
bearing precious minerals owned by me lying across and adjacent
to the proposed line of the said tunnel and for the discovery, development and possession of other and now unknown lodes and deposits
bearing and containing precious minerals; and I claim the prior right to
location of all lodes that shall or may be discovered by the construction of such tunnel for a distance of 750 feet on each side of the center
of the bore of such tunnel and along the line of such lodes or ledges
and all rights and privileges accruing to tunnel site locators by virtue
of the law in such case made and provided; size of tunnel to be five
feet wide and six and one-half feet high.  That said tunnel site is
situated in Ophir Mining District, Boise County, Idaho, and is more
particularly described as follows, to-wit:

The mouth of tunnel is situated at the base of Silver Bow Mountain, one mile north from the mouth of Stray Horse Canyon, this location stake and notice, which is situated at mouth of tunnel, is 300 feet

east of United States Mineral Monument No. 3 and is marked south center line stake No. 1 X Ray tunnel site, the proposed line and direction of said tunnel is marked and indicated on the surface as follows, to-wit: From said south center line stake running north five degrees east 500 feet to stake marked center line stake No. 2, thence north five degrees east 450 feet to stake marked center line stake No. 3, thence north five degrees east 300 feet to stake marked center line stake No. 4, thence north five degrees east 400 feet to stake marked center line stake No. 5, thence north five degrees east 500 feet to stake marked center line stake No. 6, thence north five degrees east 350 feet to stake marked center end stake No. 7, thence north five degrees east 500 feet to stake marked north center end stake No. 8, X Ray tunnel site, said last mentioned stake being situated 300 feet west of a stone monument marked the southeast corner of the Volunteer lode mining claim and 25 feet from a pine tree ten inches in diameter hewn on the side facing said stake and marked B. T. X Ray tunnel site, north end center line, thence from said point and stake running 750 feet east to corner No. 1, thence southerly 3000 feet to a stake marked corner No. 2, thence 750 feet west to location stake and notice, thence west 750 feet to corner No. 3, thence northerly 3000 feet to corner No. 1, thence east 750 feet to north center end stake, the place of beginning of the exterior boundaries of said tunnel site, each and all of the said stakes being of the size and marked as required by law.

Located this 10th day of May, 1899.

FRANK SMITH, Locator.

## AFFIDAVIT ATTACHED TO TUNNEL SITE LOCATION.

State of Idaho,     } ss.
County of Boise,    

I, Frank Smith, do solemnly swear that I am a citizen of the United States (or have declared my intention to become such) over the age of twenty-one years, that I am acquainted with the ground and claim described in the attached notice of location of tunnel site and called the X Ray tunnel site and that the same has not, nor has any part thereof been heretofore located as a tunnel site under the laws of the United States and of this State, or if so located that the same has been abandoned and forfeited by reason of the failure of such former locators to comply in respect thereto with the requirements of said laws, and that I have started work and made an excavation on said tunnel site and in said tunnel to the extent of ten feet in distance and of 160 cubic feet in quantity; that I am the identical Frank Smith, who, on the 10th day of May, 1899, located said tunnel site and claim and signed the said foregoing and attached notice of such location, and that I claim said tunnel site location by right of prior location and appropriation pursuant to law in such case made and provided. That I am prosecuting the work and construction of such tunnel for the development of lodes, veins or ledges bearing gold, silver, copper and other precious minerals, belonging to me and extending across the line of such tunnel, or within said claim, and also for the discovery and development of other, and now unknown lodes, veins or ledges and other deposits of precious minerals, lying and being along the proposed line of such tunnel and within the boundaries of said claim; that I have expended in actual work and improvements on said tunnel site and claim, not less than $100, that said tunnel has been run and constructed of full size and not less than 10 feet along the proposed line thereof, and that it is my bona fide intention to prosecute the work upon and continue the construction of said tunnel with reasonable diligence and along the line as described in the said attached notice of location and as marked on the ground in said tunnel site claim.

FRANK SMITH,

Subscribed and sworn to before me this 18th day of May, A. D. 1899.
(Seal.)                                    DOOLEY HENNESEY.

Notary Public, County of Boise.

If you desire additional ground adjacent to the mouth of your tunnel for dump surface purposes, etc., you should insert the fact in your notice of location, stating the amount and properly staking it, as, for instance, that you also claim a tract of ground 100 feet wide on each side of your tunnel and 200 feet in length, measured from the mouth of your tunnel and 200 feet in length, measured on the ground.

Question 62.    I have not worked on my tunnel site for six months. Is that an abandonment of it?

Answer.    No. But it would be considered as an abandonment of the right to all undiscovered lodes on its proposed line, should others take advantage of your neglect.

Question 63.    I have opened a blind lead in my tunnel site. Must I make a new discovery on the surface in order to locate it?

Answer.    No. The discovery in the tunnel is enough, but you should stake upon the surface, locate and record as in other lode locations, place your discovery stake as near as possible over the position of the lode, making allowance for dip of vein, stating in your notice that the lode or ledge was discovered in the tunnel, and at what distance from the mouth thereof.

Question 64.    How many lode claims can I locate on the same ledge in my own name?

Answer.    As many as you wish. The law does not limit you in this respect.

Question 65.    Suppose myself and associates locate a placer claim of one hundred and sixty acres. Can we locate another placer claim adjoining the first one located using another name and separate location for the second claim located?

Answer.    Yes and as many more as you wish whether adjoining or otherwise, provided you give a new name to each new location, mark with new boundaries and treat each claim as separate and distinct from the other. The same rule applies in case where you locate individually the 20-acre placer claim permitted by law. You may locate as many other 20-acre placer claims adjoining or otherwise or locate as many other placer claims in association with others as you desire.

Question 66.    If a placer claim embraces more than 20 acres, must I do more than $100 worth of work annually as assessment work required by law?

Answer.    No, the $100 is sufficient whether the claim embraces 20 acres or 160 acres or any subdivision thereof.

Question 67.    How shall I proceed to locate a water right for mining purposes?

Answer.    You should write to the State Engineer requesting him to send you blank application for water permit, and the necessary plats, which he will do, and such information as you require you will find printed upon these blank forms. No posting of notice is required under the present law.

**Question 68.** What constitutes a vein, lode or mineral deposit within the meaning of the mining statutes of the United States and the State of Idaho.

**Answer.** This question has been variously answered by different courts and jurists; one of the best, however, probably is that given by the eminent jurist, Judge Sawyer, in a celebrated case, as follows: "A vein or lode authorized to be located is a seam or fissure in the earth's crust filled with quartz, or with some other kind of rock in place, carrying gold, silver or other valuable mineral deposits named in the statute. It may be very thin and it may be many feet thick, or thin, in places—almost, or quite pinched out, in miners' phrase—and in other places widening out into extensive bodies of ore. So, also, in places, it may be quite, or nearly, barren, and at other places immensely rich. It is only necessary to discover a genuine mineral vein or lode, whether small or large, rich or poor, at the point of discovery within the lines of the claim located, to entitle the miner to make a valid location including the vein or lode. Its validity as a thing that may be located does not depend on what it runs."

In the case of Burke et al. vs. McDonald et al., the Supreme Court of the State of Idaho gives expression to the following: "Though to constitute a vein, it is not required that well defined walls be developed or paying ore be found within them, there must be rock, clay or earth so colored or decomposed by the mineral element as to mark and distinguish it from the inclosing country."

**Question 69.** Are mining claims treated as real estate by the laws of the State of Idaho?

**Answer.** They are.

**Question 70.** What property of a miner or prospector is exempt from execution sale under the laws of the State of Idaho?

**Answer.** The cabin or dwelling of a miner who is an actual resident of the State, which does not exceed in value the sum of five hundred dollars, also his sluices, pipes, hose, windlass, derrick, cars, pumps and tools not exceeding in value the sum of two hundred dollars, also one saddle animal and one pack animal, together with their saddles and equipments belonging to a miner actually engaged in prospecting, not exceeding in value two hundred and fifty dollars.

**Question 71.** A corporation desires to locate one hundred and sixty acres as one placer location and affixes its name as one of the locators, and the names of seven other persons as nominal locators, with the understanding that they will transfer their interests to the corporation without consideration. Would this location be valid as to the entire one hundred and sixty acres, the said seven persons being stockholders in the corporation?

**Answer.** It is very doubtful as there are numerous decisions, of both State and Federal Courts holding otherwise, and that the location would be good only to the extent of twenty acres in behalf of the corporation, the corporation being treated as one person only.

**Question 72.** In 1902, I made a valid location of the A quartz claim extending in a northeasterly and southwesterly direction and maintained my annual assessment thereon, and in 1904 while owning the same, I made a location of the B quartz claim extending in an easterly and westerly direction. The discovery and location shaft of the B claim are made within the lines of the A claim. Is the location of the B claim a valid location, all other requirements having been complied with?

Answer.            No, you can not make a new location within the lines of a pre-existing valid location, as your discovery shaft must be sunk and your notice posted on a portion of the then unappropriated mineral land of the United States, but you can amend the A location, relinquishing all rights claimed by the original location embracing that portion of B claim in conflict, and then make a new location covering the ground formerly sought to be embraced in the A location and relinquished or so much thereof as does not interfere with pre-existing valid rights.

Question 73.    In making an amended location, is it necessary for me to sink a new discovery shaft and post the amended notice on the claim?

Answer.            The Statutes of the State of Idaho are not clear on this question, but the opinion of the Author is, based upon decisions and similar statutes of other States, that if new ground is embraced within the lines of the amended location, it is necessary to sink a new discovery shaft, post the amended location notice thereat and record a substantial copy of the same within ninety days from posting, as in case of an original location, but if no new ground is embraced within the amended location and it is merely sought to correct some irregularities or defects in the original location, the Author would not consider it necessary to sink a new discovery shaft, but would advise the posting of the amended notice at or near the original discovery shaft and record a copy thereof in the office of the County Recorder, as in case of an original location.

Question 74.    In the case of amended location how long would I have after posting the amended location in which to have a copy thereof recorded?

Answer.            In this respect the Statutes of Idaho are silent, but in the opinion of the Author, you would have in a case of amended location by sinking a new discovery shaft the same time for recording as is allowed in case of an original location, to-wit: ninety days after posting an amended notice of the claim, and possibly a like period after posting amended notice in case there is no change in boundaries or new discovery shaft sunk, but would advise that no unnecessary delay be made in completing record after posting of notice.

Question 75.    In case I perform the annual assessment work for a group of claims on one of the claims, is it necessary for me to post a notice on each of the other claims, stating that the annual assessment thereon has been done on the particular claim upon which I have performed the work for the group?

Answer.            No, but the Author would advise the posting of such notice, as it would serve to render inexcusable a trespass by others without investigating, and would also advise that the fact be set forth in the affidavit of annual assessment to be filed with the County Recorder.

# INDEX.

References to Pages.